The Giving Book

a creative resource for senior high ministry

PAUL M. THOMPSON

JOANI LILLEVOLD SCHULTZ

Drawings by PEGGY HUGHES

John Knox Press
ATLANTA

All biblical quotations, unless otherwise noted, are from the *Good News Bible*, the Bible in Today's English Version. Copyright © American Bible Society, 1976. Used by permission.

Scripture quotations marked RSV are from the Revised Standard Version of the Holy Bible, copyright, 1946, 1952, and © 1971, 1973 by the Division of Christian Education, National Council of the Churches of Christ in the U.S.A. and used by permission.

"Being a Star or the Gift of Success" was printed earlier in an altered form as "A 'Star' Review" in *Resources for Youth Ministry* 14 (Winter 1982): 8–10, a quarterly publication of the Board for Youth Services of the Lutheran Church—Missouri Synod, 1333 S. Kirkwood Rd., St. Louis, MO 63122. Used by permission.

Portions of "The Gift of Strength to Face Stress" were printed earlier in "Helping Kids Handle Stress" in *GROUP* 9 (May 1983): 56–57. Reprinted by permission from GROUP Magazine, copyright 1983, Thom Schultz Publications, Inc., Box 481, Loveland, CO 80537.

The game "People to People" used in "Healing in Our Hands" (p. 86) is from MORE NEW GAMES! by Andrew Fluegelman. Copyright © 1981 by Headlands Press, Inc. Reprinted by permission of Doubleday & Company, Inc.

The quotations from Robert Raines ("The Gift of Time," p. 113) and Henry Pope Mobley ("Forever Full," p. 121) are used by permission of *The Presbyterian Outlook*, 512 E. Main St., Richmond, VA 23219; September 15, 1980 issue (Raines); April 9, 1979 issue (Mobley).

Library of Congress Cataloging in Publication Data

Thompson, Paul M., 1951–
  The giving book.

  1. Church work with youth. I. Lillevold, Joani,
1953–   . II. Title.
BV4447.T53   1985   259'.23   84-47794
ISBN 0-8042-1192-2

© copyright John Knox Press 1985
10 9 8 7 6 5 4 3 2 1
Printed in the United States of America
John Knox Press
Atlanta, Georgia 30365

DEDICATION

To the Glory of God
whose giving fills us all.

ACKNOWLEDGMENTS

We offer tribute to the people of Trinity Lutheran Church, Hudson, Wisconsin; and West-
minster Presbyterian Church, Houston, Texas;
to pastors Gene Glade, Roger Stoehr, and Woody
Berry; and to Jeanne Leland, Megs Thompson,
Sean Yancey, Shirley Sorsdal, Pam Carter, and
Dee Koza-Woodward. Thank you. Your gifts have
helped our dream become a reality.

Preface

With a unique blending of scriptural treasures and truths, *The Giving Book* provides a creative resource for those

   . . . who faithfully risk joy and struggle in working with young people,

   . . . who yearn to see God's creativity and elasticity at work,

   . . . who live adventurously—trusting, seeking, growing, and believing in the Word,

   . . . who embrace the unlimited possibilities of the Spirit, filling us with love and life-giving energy.

These pages brim with

- practical ideas
- experiential activities
- biblical truths
- relational opportunities
- creative possibilities
- fun-filled suggestions
- faith-enriching exercises.

As someone working with young people, you can expect the use of this resource

1. to create a framework where sharing beyond the normal level of conversation can occur;

2. to enable discovery of the truths of a life lived in faith;

3. to provide opportunities for growth;

4. to present biblical concepts with insight and depth bringing them to life;

5. to uniquely blend recreation, education, service, and faith experiences;

6. to enhance and supplement regular programming for young people;

7. to help build community.

This book is built upon three key concepts: God the Giver, God's gifts, and our giving. Each chapter explores one or more of these concepts and brings it to life.

The Giver

God is the life-giver, love-giver. All that life is, all that we are, comes from God who gives. John tells us, "God loved the world so much that he gave his only Son, so that everyone who believes in him may not die but have eternal life" (John 3:16). God gives, and we have eternal life—life that stretches not only across all time but deep into time. God gives, and we have moments that deepen into forevers. Our days become so full that they seem a microcosm of all life itself. The Giver moves through the world, and our horizons are expanded. Life has to be more than just the chronological coming of one day after another.

Just as God's giving transcends all that we are, it transcends all of who God is. God loved us into life and loves us through it all from before the beginning of our first day to beyond our last. Such giving is more than a string of events. Besides being what God does, giving tells us who God is—God is the Giver. Because God gives, we live.

The Gift

Within all of us lie the unique treasures that God gives. We are human beings, rich in feelings, thoughts, and actions. In faith, we acknowledge that "the Spirit's presence is shown in some way in each person for the good of all" (1 Cor. 12:7). And we recognize that "the same Spirit who does all this; as he wishes, he gives a different gift to each person" (1 Cor. 12:11). Our wealth as multifaceted and different people should be cause for celebration. Yet life and lives are easily devalued. We lose sight of these treasures. The giving and receiving of one another's gifts cannot be forgotten. Our calling is to make the world a better place. What better way can there be than opening and unwrapping the presents in one another that spark excitement, growth, and celebration? The world will benefit and God's kingdom be brought one step closer when we find and share the better of ourselves. Our presents from God can become the presence of God.

The Giving

Abundant life is love in action. We are Christ's body, and our privilege is to touch the hearts and days of those around us. Yet more than a privilege, it is a calling. We are to "offer [ourselves] as a living sacrifice to God, dedicated to his service" (Rom. 12:1*b*). And we are to "use our different gifts in accordance with the grace that God has given us" (Rom. 12:6*a*). As a people to whom much is given, we are likewise to give. Such giving needs to be expressed throughout our lives. To grow in giving is to grow in faith.

THE GIVING BOOK challenges you and those with whom you share your faith to unfold that which is deep within. It is not some new statement on faith or new work with young people but a tool that will start with your experiences and what is true for you. Use it to discover anew what you have known all along. Let it affirm once more the secret that Christ is in you. Paul Tillich once said, "Revelation is the coming together of a constellation of events: a Scripture, the time we live in, and the experience we bring to both." It is our hope that THE GIVING BOOK will unite Scripture, these times, and your experiences, so that you will transcend the ordinary and God will be revealed.

We hope that you will pick it up and become intimately involved in the sharing and discovery for which it provides. However, once you do, be prepared. Learning comes in all sizes and shapes, so expect surprises! Trusting that God works seen and unseen miracles in us can offer no less.

We offer this resource in affirmation of your God-given gifts. In the giving lies abundant joy and risk for us, for through these pages we give ourselves to you—inside out.

Joani Lillevold Schultz
Paul M. Thompson

Contents

LEADER'S GUIDE—

How to Use This Book

Having picked up this book, you have indicated your interest in one of the most exciting, challenging, and rewarding adventures in the church today. You know that ministry with young people offers the privilege to make a difference in their lives and they in yours. It holds the opportunity to let this generation discover for themselves the next chapter in God's story of love and acceptance. To those belonging to another generation, working with young people provides moments ripe with possibility for discovering the Good News again and again. It is the best way we have to provide what Hodding Carter calls "the only two lasting bequests that we can give young people: one is roots, the other wings." To help you provide the depth necessary for roots and the opportunities for hearts to soar, the following ideas are offered. May you be blessed as you pass on the good news and rise to new heights.

The Use of Time

This book differs from many others offering senior high resources in that chapters are adaptable to different time settings. A chapter can be used during a morning class, an afternoon meeting, or a special fellowship night. Several chapters can be tied together for a retreat. As the leader, you will know the most effective way for its message to be heard by your young people. However, it is important to note that the book was not planned as the sole source of programming. The chapters are best when not taken one after another but as a supplement intertwined with your regular programming. Twenty-three Sundays of THE GIVING BOOK in a row will not be as effective as one part of it every six or seven weeks.

Estimated time frames are given for each activity, but groups differ vastly in what is exciting to them. It is hard to predict which ideas will catch fire and take more time. On the other hand, when an activity does not take the time predicted, some people feel like a failure. Schedules are often unconsciously accepted as a mandate, causing people to feel rushed or panicky. Far more important than following a schedule is following interest. If something excites your group, continue with it rather than rushing through to the next activity.

Having said this, it needs to be noted that each chapter has enough material for a session of one-and-a-half to two hours. A good tip to remember in planning is to allow more time for the things that interest and excite you. Your enthusiasm will be contagious.

You as a leader will need to read the activities thoroughly before the meeting. This will help you with advance preparation. Also, with the knowledge of your group in mind, you can get a feel for how long each activity will take. With the added responsibility comes additional freedom. You can quickly conclude something that is not working or continue with a meaningful experience.

As the leader, you still may wish to place time limits on certain parts of activities. For instance, a time limit such as "you have ten minutes to do this" will often bring about a better response to a written exercise than saying, "answer these questions on your paper." The time frame can always be altered to fit the group's response. If everyone is finished after five minutes, proceed. If ten minutes is not enough time, allow for more. In this way you will be tailor-making the activity to fit your group's needs.

Similarities

Several activities in THE GIVING BOOK appear similar on the surface. Do not be fooled. Each activity is designed to fit a particular need within the context of the chapter. Part of the activity's identity comes from the context in which it is set. A second factor to consider is the assumption that the group is always the same. This is not accurate. A group of young people is a living, ever-changing entity. Rarely do you have the same people show up week after week. Those who attend are new each time, bringing their needs of the hour. They are influenced by each other as well. Ellen will talk with Greg absent but not in his presence. Because she finds him attractive, she clams up and does not know what to say. Finally, the activities in the chapters have been created with the goal of helping young people develop good, healthy self-esteem, care for one another, an understanding of the way God acts, and insight into their own behaviors. When successful, activities like this, no matter how similar or dissimilar, cannot be done too often.

Designing Activities for the Impaired

The programs offered in the chapters are not always inclusive of those with physical impairments. Because of the experiential nature of the activities, this would have been difficult. It would have necessitated designing an optional activity for each one offered. Even then there would be no guarantee that the optional activity would meet the different needs of those with different impairments. However, as the group leader or sponsor, you can be sensitive to the special needs of your young people. For instance, a visually impaired young person might need assistance with written assignments. With a little forethought and a spark of creativity, any of the activities can be modified to be inclusive. The extra effort to do so will certainly prove worthwhile.

Adapting the Material in This Book

Feel free to take what is offered between these pages and make it yours. Change it. Use a bit here and there. Bend it, blend it. In planning, do what is necessary to make the experience exciting and worthwhile. At their best, these offerings are only words. The book is complete but incomplete. What is missing is you. The most important resource you have are people, including yourself. Trust your own instincts and let this material spark your creativity. Innovate and give each activity your personal touch.

In addition to the specifics already mentioned, some general principles will be helpful if kept in mind. You will find these in the partial list of "eternal truths" that follow. Enjoy, and may God be with you as you go.

A *Partial List of "Eternal Truths"*
to Remember When Working with Young People

1. Support in a group is a two-way street. Young people will give support if you let them. It costs only your superiority.

2. Spend much time getting to know each other. Relationships, to be significant, must go beyond "hello." Sometimes hello takes far longer to finish than to say.

3. To communicate honestly, one must first share one's needs and feelings. Making yourself vulnerable by sharing ragged edges can bring surprises of great beauty. A reminder: God only needed one perfect person, and that position has already been filled.

4. If everyone is enjoying an activity and gaining something from it, so what if John fingerpaints Mary's arm!

5. Sometimes love must be given in sneak attacks, especially with teenagers. A kind word slipped in a sentence, or a hug quickly given and left, will not go unnoticed.

6. The quality of care given is not so important as the fact that it is being given. God often uses cracked pots to hold life-giving water.

7. Learn to say, "Yes! Great! Good for you! You can do it!" in fifty different ways.

8. While the activity is important, we cannot escape teaching who we are. Ultimately this is what people remember. Said another way, you and your relationships with young people say far more about God's love than the most inspired perfect activity.

9. It is good to eat and play as well as to serve and learn. All of one and none of the other makes Susie and Steve a dull girl and boy.

10. Learning is best done between equals, and all of us are equals after all.

11. Support is affirming a young person's creation or comment. Look for the good, no matter how far off the activity's planned result a response happens to be.

12. Being prepared for Sunday's meeting gives one the freedom just to be one's self. (It also greatly reduces anxiety.)

13. Caring means being with a person on a level of closeness they will allow. Nothing more, nothing less.

14. Young people offer invitations for you to agree with their negative self-concept. These invitations come in a variety of ways. You need not accept their requests to be put-down.

15. The tendency is always to underestimate your impact.

16. Avoid the "let's get the kids to do this because I want to" syndrome. It is important that young people do what they like as well as what someone thinks would be good for them.

17. The Good News is that we are valued regardless. It is still good to be valued for what we do. Recognition is the nectar of the gods to young people (and older people, too).

18. Young hearts need nurture in giving. It is a learned art, not an expected response. Patience and understanding are important ingredients.

19. Usually the highest compliment you can be given is for someone to ask to bring their friend to a meeting. What more can anyone say than, "I trust you with that which I value most"?

20. Complaining is sometimes more a reflex than a reality. A far more important measure is the interest of young people thirty minutes into the activity. Young people—all people—sometimes have fun and grow in spite of themselves.

21. If things are not going well, it never hurts to ask for help. Find a neutral party, or a friendly ear, or someone with a bit of wisdom. They will be flattered that you have asked.

22. Always, always, remember: God is with you as you go. You need only to open your eyes and see.

1

No Strings Attached

A PROGRAM
DISCOVERING LOVE
WITH NO STRINGS
ATTACHED

Materials Needed

Five snap clothes pins for each person (you could use hair clips, paper clamps, etc.)

A valuable prize for each group (possibly a picture to represent prize)

Pencil for everyone

Paper for everyone

Small box for everyone (bows on boxes?)

Index cards (so that each person has enough for everyone in the group)

Billy Joel's recording, *I Love You Just the Way You Are* (or someone to play this song with a guitar)

Record player

Love given without strings attached can be so awesome as to overwhelm us. It flies in the face of the way we understand life. You and I are products of a time that stresses a calculator mentality. What we do or do not do is added together, and we are rewarded accordingly. We are told, "You get what you pay for," or that when it comes to success, "there is no substitute for hard work." Ads suggest that we buy a certain product because we have earned it or deserve it. Even Santa Claus watches all the time and knows if we have been bad or good and weighs our worthiness in giving his presents.

No wonder a God who rewards people with no concern for what they do seems strange and out of place. Such a God is unfair. Yet, the mystery of the One who loves us in this way is not easily dismissed. We do not always understand, but we want to know more. Something about this God touches the longing buried within us to know and be known, to love and be loved, not for what we have done but for who we are. This program is designed to open young people to God's marvelously unfair love and to the gifts and Giver who gives with no strings attached.

THE GIVING BOOK

Parable Time: Workin' at the Car Wash Blues

(Estimated time: 15 minutes)

Divide the larger group into five small groups as everyone arrives. Tell the group that tonight they will be studying the unfairness of God's love and that you will be starting with a parable about five groups of workers. Assign one of the following names and identities to each of the five groups. If the group is not large enough for this many groups, you may want to eliminate one or two of the group identities.

1. *Early Birds*: this group gets up early in the morning and works hard all day.
2. *Nine-to-fives*: this group works strictly from nine-to-five.
3. *Sleep-till-nooners*: this group takes the morning easy and reports for work at noon.
4. *Free-after-threes*: this group works only part time, starting at three in the afternoon.
5. *Happy-hour-chargers*: this group has to work only one hour, from five to six.

Have each group make up a cheer to go with their identity. Explain that you are going to read a version of Matthew 20: 1–15, and that whenever they hear their group name, they are to stand up and give their cheer.

If the group has difficulty coming up with their own cheers, use the following suggestions. The *Early Birds* could all crow like roosters. The *Nine-to-fives* could whistle the first two lines of "Whistle While You Work" or sing the first line of "Working Nine to Five." Have the *Sleep-till-nooners* snore. The *Free-after-threes* could ask in unison "Are we having a car wash today?" The *Happy-hour-chargers* could imitate a bugle call to charge.

MATTHEW 20:1–15
(very paraphrased)

Plans had been made for the annual "clean your car" day at church. The event was sponsored by the youth group, who planned to raise money for their upcoming summer trip. Pam, the senior high worker, had gotten out the publicity and made sure all the buckets, brushes, sponges, hoses, and soap were gathered. She promised each person who worked at the car wash $25 worth of credit for the trip.

The April day came, clear and warm, perfect for washing cars and a welcome change after the dreary winter rains. When the *Early Birds* arrived, cars were already in line and waiting. They dove into their task with vigor, but the line continued to grow. Still, the *Early Birds* worked. Pam worried that she might have done too well on the publicity.

At 8:30 she called another group of the young people to come help. Since it was still early in the day, she promised them the full $25, too. They agreed to be there at 9 o'clock. Sure enough, the *Nine-to-fives* showed up right on time. The *Early Birds* were glad. The *Nine-to-fives* were a big help.

But the line of muddy cars continued to stretch. No matter how fast the sponges moved and the soapsuds flew, it didn't seem to matter. Pam knew what she had to do. She went into the church and called the group that had stayed out late for last night's high school dance. After they were told the problem and promised $25 worth of credit, the *Sleep-till-nooners* came and started work right beside the *Nine-to-fives*. The *Early Birds* were glad to see the *Sleep-till-nooners* arrive.

The *Sleep-till-nooners* made a contribution, but it was not helping. Cars lined up across the church parking lot and out into the street. By now the *Nine-to-fives* had shriveled fingers. Pam needed reinforcements. She searched the group list and called a few of the people who were supposed to be there but hadn't shown up. "Why aren't you helping?" she inquired. "Nobody asked us," they said, "but we are free after three and would like to go on the trip, and the $25 sure would help." So, the *Free-after-threes* came to the church and worked.

Well, folks, the *Early Birds*, the *Nine-to-fives*, *Sleep-till-nooners*, and the *Free-after-threes* washed more cars than they could count. You might say the car wash was a splash hit. Dirty, dusty vehicles were transformed. Still they came. Pam was worried about whether or not they could wash all of the cars.

Finally, she called everyone else on the youth group list and promised to give them a $25 credit if they would help. This last group, the *Happy-hour-chargers*, showed up at 5 o'clock. The *Happy-hour-chargers* worked with the *Nine-to-fives* and the *Free-after-threes* worked with the *Early Birds*, and the *Sleep-till-nooners* worked with everyone.

With the *Happy-hour-chargers'* help, the last car was finally washed. As it sparkled out of sight, Pam called the group together. She got out her book, and as everyone stood around her, she gave them their due. Pam gave $25 worth of credit to the *Early Birds*, $25 to the *Nine-to-fives*, $25 to the *Sleep-till-nooners*, $25 to the *Free-after-threes*, and $25 to the *Happy-hour-chargers*.

With their $25 receipt in hand, the *Early Birds* began to grumble. "We don't mean to be in a fowl mood, but we *Early Birds* worked a lot harder and longer than these *Nine-to-fives*, these lazy *Sleep-till-nooners*, these free-loading *Free-after-threes*, and certainly these hopeless *Happy-hour-chargers*. Why, they hardly washed a windshield! Where were the *Free-after-threes* when that

THE GIVING BOOK

big truck came through this morning? Pam, you sure don't know much about business!"

"Listen, folks," Pam answered. "I promised $25 worth of credit to the *Happy-hour-chargers*, $25 to the *Free-after-threes*, $25 to the *Sleep-till-nooners*, $25 to the *Nine-to-fives*, and I promised $25 to the *Early Birds*. I haven't cheated you. We made an agreement. I want to give everyone this much. Are you jealous because I'm generous?"

So they all went home with their $25 credit for the trip in their hands.

Understanding I | *God's love is unfair.*

Prizes and Surprises
(Estimated time: 20 minutes)

For the next activity you may wish to keep the same groups or redivide into three slightly larger groups. If necessary, wear different colored name tags to identify groups. You will need five snap clothes pins for each person and a valuable prize for each of the groups. The prizes should be something tangible that the group would value and really like to have.

Give each person five clothes pins. Explain that you are going to play a game. The object is to get rid of the clothes pins each group has. A player may get rid of his or her clothes pins by pinning them on someone else's clothing who is not a member of his or her group. If someone puts a pin on your clothing, you can take it off and try to pin it on someone else. At the end of five minutes, time will be called and the team with the fewest clothes pins, either in their hands or pinned on them, will be the winner.

Show the teams what the prize will be before the game starts, but show only one prize and explain that there will be only one prize given. Do not show the other prizes you have and keep them out of sight. Do not be afraid to emphasize the prize as you show it. If you choose a prize such as a privilege like an expense-paid trip for hamburgers or something similar, be sure to have a picture or something to represent it.

Start the game. At the conclusion of five minutes, stop the mania and determine the winner. Have an elaborate awards ceremony. Then start to go on to the next activity, but say, "Oh, wait! I almost forgot we have a prize for the group who came in second." There will be some discussion since this is a change in what you have already stated. Have the same awards ceremony and give an identical prize. Repeat the procedure for the other group again, giving the identical prize.

After all the prizes have been awarded, divide again into different small groups of up to eight people to discuss and debrief the experience. Make sure that every group has representatives from each of the competing groups so that the variety of experiences can be shared. You will need to stay in these groups for the remainder of the activities. Possible discussion questions include:

1. How did you feel during the awards ceremony?
2. Did you think the experience was a fair one? Why or why not?
3. Did you feel guilty taking the prize if you didn't finish first? Explain?
4. Do you see any parallel between the game and the Bible passage?

After the groups are finished have one person from each group report on their discussion.

Understanding II | *We are loved no matter what.*

Unconditional Love

(Estimated time: 20 minutes)

Explain to the group that not only is God's love unfair but that it comes without expectations. Tell them that in the next activity an attempt will be made to discover some of this God-like love here on earth. Make sure everyone has a paper and pencil. On their paper, have the participants make the following chart.

	Two Years Ago	Now	Future
I love			
They love me			

Next, explain that they are to fill in the chart, listing on the top half of the page the five people whom they love most for each of the times given. Then they are to list on the bottom half of the page the five people who love or loved them the most for each of the times. Point out that people can be listed in more than one place on the chart.

Once this is done, use several of the questions listed below for small group discussion.

1. Are there any people who are in all six slots? If so, describe them.
2. Are there any noticeable absences of people you thought should be included, but are not, e.g., parents, brothers, sisters?
3. Which time was easier to fill out, and why?

4. Is the love unfair that you give these people or that they give you?
5. Are there any people listed whose love you have to earn?
6. Do these people love you no matter what you do or in spite of what you do?
7. Talk about a time when you were loved unconditionally by one of these people.
8. Talk about a time when you unconditionally loved one of these people.

Presents from Presence
(Estimated time: 15 minutes)

For the next activity, you will need a small box for each person and enough index cards or slips of paper so that each person has one for every other member of the small group. The activity is enhanced if the boxes have bows and name tags on them so they look like gifts. Place the boxes in the center of each group.

Have each small group member complete the following sentence about the other small group members, putting one on each card:

> A present you give me from your presence is your . . .

Stress that you would like them to include qualities of the people such as their warmth, care, friendliness, as opposed to something the people do like play basketball or make good grades.

Once the cards have been completed, they should be placed in the individual's box. Then have a member of the group take another member's gift box to them. The person who brings the box to them opens it and shares what the group has written. The group may add comments as this is done. Take turns among the group in presenting the boxes. After all the boxes have been opened and shared, they may be taken home for other times when the person would like to remember the presents from his or her presence.

Closing Worship
(Estimated time: 5 minutes)

Pray, thanking God for those people who love us without strings attached. Offer prayers of gratitude for the privilege of loving this way. Close by playing Billy Joel's recording of "I Love You Just the Way You Are." Better still, have someone from the group play this with a guitar. Preface the song by saying, "Just for a moment I would like you to get comfortable and close your eyes. Imagine that this song is God's word for you."

2

The Nonsense of Giving

Time and time again, people who work with young people in churches throw up their hands. The frustration is at the apparent lack of a giving spirit among the group. "All this group wants to do is play; they are not interested in any kind of Christian service" and "This might as well be the YWCA for all the commitment these young people have" are all-too-common statements. On the surface it would seem that these attitudes are correct.

When we take a deeper look, several ideas begin to emerge. They shed new light on an old problem. First, giving represents a very complex form of behavior. It may arise from various motivations; guilt, joy, fear, the need to impress, or to offer a bargain. Giving may come at great cost or no cost at all. It requires recognition of a desire and the decision to act upon that feeling. We may think we simply give, but our generosity represents the end of a chain of activity. Second, giving is learned. With all its complexity, we cannot expect young people to show up on Sunday afternoon enthusiastically ready to do a project the sponsors thought appropriate. Like anything learned, giving takes practice. It must arise from a desire within those who are sharing.

Third, giving has a strange but often forgotten paradox. The good news of giving does not seem necessarily good. "You mean I am going to have to give up something and that's supposed to make me feel good?" How can taking something away, doing with less time, less money, or resources make a person feel better? It is our natural inclination to get rather than to give.

This is illustrated by the story of an old Arkansas farmer. The Reverend went to talk to him. He said, "Brother Jones, if you had two farms, wouldn't you be willing to give one to the Lord?" The farmer replied, "Certainly I would, Reverend Brown." "And if you had $10,000, wouldn't you be willing to give $5,000 to the Lord?" the preacher inquired. "Certainly I would." The minister went on, "And if you had two pigs, wouldn't you be willing to give one of them to the Lord?" The farmer responded, "Now, wait a minute!. That's not fair! Reverend Brown, you know I have two pigs."

When we look at giving in terms of doing with less, the good news is not so good. Yet giving holds a joy and fulfillment not otherwise known. Responding to God's grace and generosity brings a happiness that cannot be achieved through more self-centered activities. When we give love away, we end up having more.

In sharing the "Good News," giving and receiving become mixed and mingled in beautiful ways. Perhaps for you it happened in a unique gift you lovingly gave a friend. Maybe the blending occurred when just being there meant as much to you as the person with whom you stayed. Wherever the joy of giving happens, we need to take note. Let us celebrate love's delightful idiosyncrasy, the co-mingling of giving and receiving. Too often this discovery is never made.

This chapter provides a chance to practice giving. At the same time, it opens the door for giving to be intermingled with wonder.

AN EVENT LOOKING
AT THE NONSENSE
OF GIVING

Materials Needed
Apple for each person
Cassette tape recorder and tape
Secret Servant information sheets
Envelopes
Pencils or pens
Paper

Secret Servants: Mission Possible
(Estimated time: 15 minutes)

You will want to meet with young people to prepare one week before the activities suggested below. It will be necessary to have an apple for each person, a cassette tape recorder, copies of the Secret Servant sheet found in this chapter, envelopes, and a cassette containing the message that follows. Give people the Secret Servant information sheets. Once the sheets have been completed, instruct the group to put their individual sheets into envelopes and seal them. Then have the young people place a letter of the alphabet on the outside of the envelope without letting anyone else see it. Any letter will do. Collect the envelopes and shuffle them.

SECRET SERVANT INFORMATION SHEET

NAME _____

ADDRESS _____

THINGS I LIKE _____

_____

_____

THINGS I DON'T LIKE _____

_____

_____

FAVORITE: FLAVOR _____

                 COLOR _____

                 SPORT _____

                 ACTIVITY _____

Play the tape for the group with this recorded message

(begin with music that suggests a secret mission): Your mission, should you choose to accept it, is to become a secret servant for a week. As a secret servant, you are to do two things. First, when you leave you will be given an apple. You are to give this apple to someone who is special to you. Tell the person that you were instructed to give the apple away to someone who is special, and he or she is the person whom you picked. Be ready to report on what happens when we meet next week.

The second thing you are to do must be done in *absolute secrecy*. When you leave you will be given an envelope. Check the letter on the outside and make sure it is not the one you put on an envelope. If it happens to be, return that envelope and you will get another. Do not open the envelope until you get home. Tell no one of its contents. I repeat, no one.

For the next week you will be the secret servant of the person revealed in the envelope. How you carry out your mission is up to you, but you must give them at least three gifts. Your apple is not to be one of them. You may write them notes, do things for them, provide a small gift, but whatever you do, your identity must remain anonymous. In order to confuse your target, it may be necessary to give gifts or to do things for other people so that secret servant identities remain a secret. Keep your identity secret. Repeat. A secret. If you are caught, we here at headquarters will deny any knowledge of you. Good luck on this risky and dangerously exciting mission. This tape will self-destruct in 60 seconds. (music)

Give people an envelope and an apple when they leave.

Give-a-Hug Game

(Estimated time: 20 minutes)

Start the next week's activities by playing the give-a-hug or back-rub game. Choose whether you wish to give hugs or back rubs. Begin by saying, "Give a hug to someone wearing blue." The young people are then to find someone wearing blue and hug them. Continue, using the following categories, or make up your own. Make sure everyone gets several hugs. Give a hug to

Someone in band	Someone wearing a watch
Someone not from your school	Someone wearing glasses
Someone wearing tennis shoes	Someone wearing a ring
Someone taller than you	Someone in the eleventh grade
Someone you've wanted to hug	Someone with pierced ears
Someone of the same sex	Someone with brown eyes
Someone of the opposite sex	Someone born this month

Understanding I | *We who know the joy of receiving tend to lose the joy of giving.*

A Blessed-to-Give Bible Study

(Estimated time: 15 minutes)

Read part of Paul's farewell address to the Ephesian elders found in Acts 20:22–38. Pay particular attention to verse 35. Ask the group to answer the following questions.

1. Is "it is more blessed to give than to receive" a truth about life or commandment? (Let the young people give reasons why they think one way or the other.)
2. Share a time when you found it more blessed to give than to receive.
3. Do you see yourselves primarily as a giver or receiver? Why?

Understanding II | *In true sharing, the giving and receiving become intermingled.*

Servant Experiences
(Estimated time: 20 minutes)

Have people share their experiences with the apple and as secret servants. Go around the room taking turns, and let people reveal their secret servants. Take plenty of time; let people talk about the feelings they had while giving. Was it fun, joyous, exciting? Was it frustrating? If the experience was fun, what made this giving that way compared to others? Point out instances where the giving and receiving became intermingled.

Understanding III | *God calls us to give of ourselves.*

Project: Giver
(Estimated time: 15 minutes)

Have a time of planning and promising to give to those in need. Ask the group to think of situations they know about that have real needs. Encourage people to commit to themselves to give to someone in need.

Plan a group giving activity. It may be a church work day; a surprise party giving recognition to a special teacher, pastor, or friend; a project in an area nursing home. Pick a project that can be completed in a specific time-frame rather than an ongoing one. The less experienced your group is in giving, the more important it becomes for the project to have results that can be seen. Above all, let the giving activity come from a need the group feels. To help with time, a list of tips for service projects with young people is included at the end of this chapter.

Worship
(Estimated time: 5 minutes)

Close with a prayer. Thank God for the gifts we have been given. Ask God for help in being a giver and in fulfilling the promises we have made to ourselves earlier. Sing an appropriate song, such as "Pass It On" or "They Will Know We Are Christians by Our Love."

3

When Imitation Is a Virtue

A CHANCE TO SEE
THAT WE ARE MADE
IN GOD'S IMAGE

Materials Needed

Sheet of paper for each person

Pens

Markers

Scissors for each person

Construction paper

Thumb tacks

Bulletin board

Bibles

Camera (Polaroid or any one
    that instantly develops) for
    each small group

Poster board for each group

Glue or tape

A photographer showed a friend a collection of favorite photos. One particularly beautiful shot captured a magnificent sunset reflected in a lake. The oranges and azures blended softly, creating a vision of beauty and serenity. After the friend had expressed admiration, the photographer smiled mischievously and turned the picture around in her guest's hands. With the lake mirroring heaven, it was difficult to tell which was earth and which was sky. To the guest's surprise, she had admired the work of art while holding it upside down.

We often see our images similarly twisted. We see ourselves as too fat, too short, too sensitive, too shy, too young, too old, or too something. We invert our images, placing our inadequacies at the top of the list. Our intended image somehow gets turned upside down. This comes as little surprise. Many influences stir our imagination about what a perfect image is and whisper continuously of our inability to make the grade. If we were to remain surface people, these perceptions of ourselves would be sufficient. But our faith calls us to deeper answers.

Though we are quick to forget, we are made in God's image. In Genesis the Hebrew word used for image literally means something that is cut out. We are cut out of the same material as God. We share with God the ability to communicate, to think, even the ability to transcend ourselves. We know goodness, hope, care, and love with God. Even with these qualities, we are still human and far less than God. The original meaning of image was that of imitation. Imitation becomes a virtue when we recall the Original in whose image we are made. Now is the time to untwist and turn aright our images.

An imitation, while never quite equaling the original, still has value of its own. These activities offer you the promise found in knowing we are made in God's image.

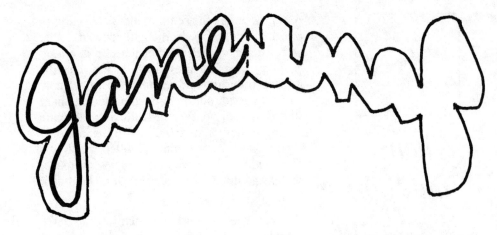

Name Reflections
(Estimated time: 10 minutes)

Give each person a sheet of construction paper, pen, or marker, and a pair of scissors. Ask group members to fold the construction paper in half and write their names on the paper. The letters of the name should touch the crease. The bigger the letters the better. Then use scissors to cut out the name, being careful not to cut on the crease so that a mirror image of the name is formed. Put these on the bulletin board or meeting room wall. Tell the group you will be making discoveries about images and what it means to be created in God's image.

Understanding I | Our images have many different facets.

My Image
(Estimated time: 15 minutes)

Give members a sheet of paper. Have them divide it into four parts with the pen or marker used in the earlier activity. In one part young people draw their "image" as they see it at home. Use the remaining three parts to do the same for school, church, and with friends. When these are complete, have them draw what they imagine God's image of them to be on the back of the paper. Use crayons or felt markers to provide more color.

Divide into small groups and discuss the "images." Ask "are the images different for various places or the same? Why are they different? Does a difference cause conflict, or is it helpful?"

Understanding II | *We forget we are made in God's image.*

God's Image
(Estimated time: 10 minutes)

Give each small group an RSV Bible and have them read Genesis 1:27. Ask the groups to talk about what it means to be made in God's image. Discuss what is easiest and most difficult to believe about being created in this way. See if the groups can reach a consensus as to what parts of our humanity are made in God's image, e.g., parents' care, being oneself, the ability to think or feel, etc.

Understanding III | *We are called to see ourselves in many different ways, yet we are always the same, created in God's image.*

Picturing God's Image
(Estimated time: 60 minutes)

Give each small group a camera that develops pictures instantly. Tell the groups that they have one hour to photograph people who represent being made in God's image. The groups may choose to pose for the pictures, or they may photograph other people. In taking the photos, groups may wish to drive around the city. If you anticipate this, have adequate transportation and a sponsor to drive each group. The groups then come back and make a poster or collage using their photographs. Entitle it "Made in God's Image." Have groups share their creations with each other.

For a closing, pray, giving thanks for being made in God's image. Ask God for help to keep us ever mindful of this gift.

When Imitation Is a Virtue

4

Forgiving— Creating a World Without Walls

It is the most closely-guarded wall in the world. Those on either side watch with great diligence and keen eyes. Naturally, with such scrutiny, skirmishes break out frequently. A person on one side tries to get to the other. When a violation occurs, retaliation is swift. The wall of which we speak is the imaginary one that divides the back seat of the car during summer vacations. How many miles you and I have spent listening to "Mom, she's on my side! Get her off. I don't want your cootie-coated fingers on my side! I saw that foot! Mom!" If the story of Cain and Abel were told today, it would take place not near Eden, but in a Datsun.

We smile patronizingly at these most innocent of walls. After all, as long as we're not involved, we think it's cute. Besides, we've outgrown such silliness. But have we gotten so far from the silliness, the sadness of it all? Walls are very much with us.

The woman stops at the entrance of a church. For her, the sun creates a silent but dazzling moment. Its light graces the elegant stained glass at just the right angle. The wind gently touches her hair. She turns away from the bejeweled window and looks almost wistfully at the great cathedral. She wants to enter, but she cannot. The steps form a barrier and may as well be a wall. Her hands begin to work in lean movement, the wasted motion eliminated by countless repetitions. Silently she rolls her wheel chair away from the steps.

Half a world away, a city is divided by a monument to distrust. In three hundred miles, the Berlin Wall contains enough wire to circle the globe three times. Doubt and suspicion have poured enough concrete to insure the separation of friends and family.

Yet these are the simpler of the walls that separate us from each other and from God's intended way. They are in the open, obvious and tangible. Far more difficult to scale are the invisible walls created around our hearts, walls that hold back, hide, and divide. A word is spoken in anger, and two people go unreconciled. A brick is lowered into place. You and I cheat, and no one discovers. The act supplies another brick. A lack of concern for those in need provides the mortar. A deception that is easier to live with than to explain gives still another brick. The wall building continues until we feel isolated, alienated.

For as long as God has been around, God has been concerned with tearing down the walls that would keep us apart. In a like way, we the church are called to work at removing barriers that separate humans from God and from each other. To fulfill our calling of reconciliation, God has shared the valuable gift of forgiveness.

Forgiving. God has always been *for* giving. But what does that mean? Is "for" used to mean in spite of, like "he is not very bright *for* all his learning?" Is for-giving a giving that occurs in spite of everything we do and are? Or is "for" used to mean in place of, like "she used a book for a paperweight?" For-giving is God giving love in place of our inadequate expressions of care. The "for" of forgiving is actually an Anglo-Saxon prefix that originally meant "too much." Forgiving is God's giving too much love over what we ever earn or deserve. When God or we love more deeply than another deserves, walls crumble and cannot stand. This is what we are to do, to be wall breakers instead of wall makers.

Walls were put around ancient cities to keep undesirables out. Perhaps God's interest in breaking down walls comes from the fact that for God there are no undesirables. May this activity be a beginning for you in creating a world without walls where all are desired and loved.

A PROGRAM ENABLING YOUNG PEOPLE TO BEGIN CREATING A WORLD WITHOUT WALLS

Materials Needed

Stacks of old newspapers

A roll of masking tape for every three persons

A garbage bag for every three persons

Understanding I | *Sin separates us from God and each other.*

Building Walls
(Estimated time: 35 minutes)

You will need to have stacks of old newspapers, a roll of masking tape, and a garbage bag for every three young people for this activity.

As participants arrive, give every three people a stack of newspapers and some masking tape. Tell them that their task is to build a wall to separate them from everyone else in the group. Suggest making paper tubes for bars or taping sheets together to create a curtain or a wall. While they must remain in the meeting room, they can creatively use anything in the room to help them, e.g., chairs, walls, tables, etc. See who can best hide from the rest.

Once people are behind their "walls," share the purpose of the time together. Say something like, "we are going to discover and experience the joy of forgiveness. But before we can celebrate, we need to recognize our short-comings and failures as God's people. Sin separates. Walls of sin can keep us from relationships that could be. For the next few moments, imagine that the walls you have created are walls that alienate you and keep you from one another."

Have each group choose one "wall-maker" that they feel separates one person from another. Examples that might be offered include cheating, hating, cursing, lying, pride, stealing, etc. When everyone has selected their "wall-maker," choose one person to be in an open space between the walls to speak the "wall-breaker" word: "FORGIVEN."

Begin with that person in the room softly saying, "FORGIVEN," while all the others join, one by one, saying their "wall-makers." Bit by bit, the sounds of sin will appear to cover up "FORGIVEN," yet all the while "FORGIVEN" continues to be spoken. The "wall-makers" will gradually become louder. Now, reverse the chants' volume, and eliminate the "wall-makers" chanting, one by one until "FORGIVEN" is the final word that is heard. Someone will have to serve as "choral director," signaling people to begin and cease chanting, to get louder and then softer.

| *Understanding II* | *Forgiveness removes the barriers that separate us from God.* |

Read Ephesians 2:14. Afterward, continue by saying, "Christ is the ultimate wall-breaker. Let us rejoice that we are the ones God uses today as wall-breakers. God speaks the good word of forgiveness through each of us."

While still in groups of three behind the paper walls, have each individual share with that small group a "wall-maker" that is a painful part in his or her life. Encourage young people to share times when they felt separated from others by sin. After one person shares a confession, the other two are to offer words of forgiveness and care. (You may need to supply a few phrases that express forgiveness, such as "Skip, God loves you still. You are forgiven.") When all three have finished sharing, celebrate "wall-breaking." Tear down the newspaper walls and stuff them into garbage bags. Set the garbage bags aside for later use.

| *Understanding III* | *God searches us out and forgives us, no matter what the barriers may be.* |

Once the young people have torn down their walls and put them in garbage bags, prepare the group for the next activity by using words similar to the following: "Often we spend more time making walls than breaking walls. The result is that sometimes we feel lost and alienated. We become keenly aware of our separateness and our estrangement from others. It may seem as if we are in one place and everyone else is in another. To discover God's response to us when we lose ourselves, we will look at one of the parables of Jesus."

An Echo Pantomine Parable

(Estimated time: 30 minutes)

Below you will find the story of the shepherd and the lost lamb done in an echo pantomine. Have the group say and do whatever the leader says and does. Everyone should be standing.

THE SHEPHERD AND THE LOST LAMB
(an echo pantomine paraphrasing Luke 15:1–7)

One day when many tax collectors and other outcasts came to listen to Jesus, the Pharisees and the teachers of the law started grumbling, "This man welcomes outcasts and even eats with them!" So Jesus told them a parable.

It may have gone something like this (repeat after me the words I say and the actions I do):

Words	Actions
I'm a shepherd.	Both hands point to self.
And believe me	Raise one finger to make a point.
it's not an easy job!	Wipe brow.
My flock of sheep is huge!	Spread arms wide.
But I keep a *very* close count. One, two, three, four, five, six, seven, eight, nine, ten.	Hold up all ten fingers, count each finger deliberately, count each finger deliberately.
We travel for days	Mark time for marching in place and use a sweeping motion with the arms to denote a wide area.
near flowing streams	Kneel and make a rippling motion with hands to represent stream.
to drink cool water.	Cup hands, slurp, and say, "ahhh."
We cross rocky places	Mark time in place again, stepping very gingerly.
and dangerous ridges	Stand on tiptoes, trying to keep balance.
to rolling grassy hillsides.	Outline imaginary hillside.
No matter what	Wave arms in horizontal crossing manner.
we stick together.	Clasp hands together.
For I love my sheep	Outstretch arms.
and they love me!	Fold arms and hug chest.

But there are "baaad" days.	Shake head "no" and fold arms in front.
If *one* lamb strays away	Shooing motion away.
I could leave it behind	Extend one arm, palm out.
and pretend I didn't notice.	Turn head in opposite direction from extended arm.
What's one lamb?	Shrug shoulders.
But a good shepherd	Point thumb toward self.
looks high	Stand on tiptoes, hands above eyes searching.
and low.	Stoop down, hands still above eyes, looking in both directions.
And listens for the faint sounds.	Make whispering noise with hands cupped by ear.
That little lamb can't pull the wool over my eyes.	Pull an imaginary window blind down over the eyes.
I'll search everywhere	Look in all directions, hands above eyes.
until I find the lamb!	Arms wide open.
Then I'll cradle it	Cradle an imaginary lamb.
and hold it close.	Fold arms and hug lamb.
I'll put it on my shoulders	Put imaginary lamb on shoulders.
and carry it back home.	Mark time in place while holding imaginary lamb on shoulder.
I'll gather my friends	Gathering motion with arms toward self.
and we'll celebrate!	Leap in the air with arms up and out.
In the same way	Arms at side.
when one sinner seeks forgiveness out of ninety-nine righteous	Point finger for one, make wide, sweeping motions with arms.
there's great joy in heaven!	Arms reach heavenward.

Talk about the parable using the questions below:

1. Have you ever been lost and then found? Share your feelings about the experience.

2. Have you ever helped someone find themselves? If so, how? Talk about it.
3. Has someone ever helped you find yourself? What was the experience like?
4. The passage in the Bible talks about repenting. When we repent or are forgiven, does the action start with us or with God?
5. What does forgiveness say about God? What does our need for forgiveness say about us?
6. Is God like the shepherd in the parable? How or how not?

A Reconciliation Experience
(Estimated time: 10 minutes)

To experience reconciliation in a visual way, gather the group in a circle for worship. Have them place their arms around each other. The leader begins by talking about the enjoyment and pleasure of being a part of a group and sharing the closeness that a group offers. The leader then acknowledges that while the potential for being a real group and sharing closeness with each other always exists, sometimes we separate ourselves and can't enjoy the love God intends. The leader continues by saying, "To show you what I mean, I would like everyone in the circle who has been a part of a group and has ever let that group down, to drop your arms from another's shoulders." After a brief period of silence, the leader continues the activity as follows:

Leader Says	Action
Sometimes we say things that are harmful to other people.	I would like anyone who has ever said something that was harmful to another member of a group to take a step backward.

Silence

Often we exclude others from our group.	If anyone has ever excluded another person from a group or made someone feel left out, please take another step backward.

Silence

Sometimes we say things that aren't true. We deny making a mistake, or we are afraid to tell somebody something.	If this has ever happened to you, I would like you to turn and face away from the center of the circle.

Silence

Sometimes we have pretended not to see the needs of other people.

If there have been times that you have ignored the needs of other people and remained apart from them, I would like you to close your eyes.

Silence

We were meant to be together, yet at times our actions keep us apart.

If you have ever helped someone with a need they had, I would like you to turn around.

Silence

It is important to listen to people.

If you have ever taken the time to listen to a friend who had a problem, I would like you to take one step in toward the circle.

Silence

The best gift we can give people is to welcome them and make them feel included.

If you have ever made someone feel welcome and a part of things, open your eyes.

Silence

Confession to one another can tear down walls.

If you have ever shared a way that you have failed someone, even if it was hard to do, then take another step in toward the circle.

Silence

God asks us to forgive one another.

If you have ever forgiven someone, then place your arms around the people beside you.

A group hug would be an appropriate ending.

Playful Celebration
(Estimated time: 15 minutes)

As a closing, the group can celebrate together by playing volleyball with one of the stuffed garbage bags. A game requiring less space would be a circle toss. One of the garbage bags is batted back and forth in a circle. The object is to keep the garbage bag from touching the ground.

5

Giving God Our Best

AN ACTIVITY
LOOKING AT
THE PARABLE OF
THE TALENTS

Materials Needed

Two pair of long, white gloves

Two large gold-colored rings

Copies of the script

Stage (black background cloth, several tables, skirt of black cloth or paper)

Spotlight

Pencils

Paper

Olive oil in bowl

In the late afternoons, television stations occasionally offer a rerun entitled "The Six-Million Dollar Man." The name comes from the lead character who, after an accident, is rebuilt through the miracles of biomedical engineering. He is then worth six million dollars. In an afternoon daydream aided by an old television program, such a clear, concise estimate of one's worth is plausible. With the gray glimmer of a world behind the glass screen, it is even possible to believe a person is worth six million dollars.

Most of us lack the luxury of such clarity. We are told that we have worth because God made us. Hearing of our worth is one thing, but believing it is another matter entirely. One of the ironies of the Christian faith is that our struggle does not come so much from believing or not believing in God but accepting what God believes about us.

Even more important than the question of our worth is what worth we will bring to what we have been given. God has given us talents, abilities, and a world in which to use them. When we stare into that great expanse of life, what do we see? What do we make out of car wrecks and earthquakes and babies starving? How do we make sense of the nuclear arms race, the space race, struggles for freedom, and battles with cancer? How do we make the full use of our talents? Where do we fit in this cosmic expanse of agony and opportunity? The vastness of the vision can overwhelm us. What do we make of life?

The choice is ours. While God owns everything, God has entrusted it to us. We can affirm with the Psalmist, "that the earth is the LORD's and the fullness thereof; the world, and they that dwell therein" (24:1, KJV). At the same time, we must remember that while the world is not ours, it is our responsibility. It is remarkable! We love a God who creates such a majestic place as the earth, authors the breath-taking wonder of relationships, and then turns all of this over to us. God is either foolhardy or incredibly trusting. Sometimes there is not much difference between the two.

In Matthew 25 Jesus tells a parable about a master who gives a sum of money to each of his servants, each according to his abilities. The one who draws the master's ire is the one-talent servant. At first it seems out of character for Jesus. Jesus has spent his life including the most doubtful people—Zacchaeus, quiet Andrew playing second fiddle to Peter, a blind beggar. Why does he now strike out at the one given the short end of things? It is precisely from this same care. The one-talent servant was far too quick to accept his limitations and deny God's gifts. He felt he didn't have much and was of no great importance to anyone, even to God. Why should he try? God calls us to be no less than our best. We cannot hide behind the clouds of our self-doubt and questioning.

God creates miracles with one-talent people who believe enough in God to believe in themselves and their importance. Again the issue is not how much we have but what we do with what we have. These activities offer a way to reflect on the use of our talents.

| Understanding I | *God uses our talents and has high expectations of us.* |

Getting Started

A "Handy" Parable of the Talents
(Estimated time: 20 minutes)

Several weeks before you wish to do this activity, select the young people to participate in the hand puppet parable. At least three people are necessary, one to be the reader and a minimum of two to do the hand motions. To include more, several people can read, and up to four persons can do the hands. Others can work on the "set" or stage. If only two people are used for the hands, have one person be the master and the two-thousand-coin person. The other person's hands will be the five-thousand-coin and the one-thousand-coin persons.

The hand parable does not require great amounts of practice or an elaborate set but will go much more smoothly if the young people have been through it several times and are familiar with the motions. The parable may also be used in a worship experience with the congregation.

Materials needed for the parable: (1) two pair of long white gloves, (2) two large obvious gold-colored rings to be worn by the master, (3) copies of the script, (4) a stage. If a puppet stage is not available, a simple stage can be created by using a black background cloth placed on a wall and several tables. Set up one table normally. Place the other table on its side on top of the first table so that the table top faces the audience and hides the actors. Card tables and typical church tables work well. Put a skirt of black cloth or paper around the bottom of the table to block the audience's view of the participants. Only the hands should be seen. You can enhance the hands by putting them in direct light and darkening the area where the audience will sit. Use a spotlight or any other light that can be directly focused on the stage area.

As the young people arrive, tell them that today they are going to explore one of Jesus' teachings in a new way.

THE PARABLE OF THE TALENTS
Matthew 25:14–30

The parable begins with the audience seeing one set of hands, the master hand and the two-thousand-coin hand. The hands are clasped with fingers interlocked as if someone is praying. (Master Hand = MH, Five-Thousand-Coin Hand = 5TH, Two-Thousand-Coin Hand = 2TH, and One-Thousand-Coin Hand = 1TH.)

The Story	*The Actions*
The kingdom of heaven will be like this.	MH and 2TH unfold, putting palms up and outward. Then 2TH drops from sight.
Once there was a man	MH points one finger upward.
who was about to leave on a trip.	MH waves goodbye to the audience.
He called his servants	MH uses one finger and makes a motion to "come here."
and put them in charge of the property.	MH points to the audience like Uncle Sam saying, "I want you."

He gave to each one according to his abilities.	5TH, 2TH, and 1TH hands come up, palm up and open, waiting to be filled.
To one he gave 5,000 silver coins.	MH counts on fingers slowly—one, two, three, four, five—then lightly slaps the open palm of the 5TH. Then the 5TH hand disappears.
To another he gave 2,000 silver coins.	MH repeats above, only this time counting to two. Then 2TH disappears.
To another he gave 1,000 silver coins.	MH repeats the above, this time counting one. Then 1TH disappears.
And then he left on his trip.	MH turns sideways to the audience and marches across the stage going slightly up and down until it reaches side stage and then MH disappears.
The servant who had received 5,000 coins went at once and invested his money	5TH comes up open and dancing, waving five fingers. The hand closes suddenly, with the index finger pointed up like, "I have an idea." The 5TH disappers.
The servant who had received 5,000 coins earned another 5,000.	5TH and 1TH come up flashing ten fingers by opening and closing the hands rapidly. Then 5TH and 1TH stand palm to palm with fingers not interlocked. Hands disappear.
In the same way the servant who had received 2,000 coins	2TH appears with two fingers extended like a peace symbol.
earned another 2,000 coins.	1TH comes up in a fist and lightly hits the side of the 2TH and two fingers pop up on 1TH. Both 1TH and 2TH flash two fingers rapidly by extending and drawing in the fingers. Then the two fingers on each hand hug each other in victory. 2TH and 1TH then disappear.
But the servant who had received 1,000 coins	1TH comes up with one finger up and turns as if looking around.

went off	1TH marches across stage area.
dug a hole in the ground	5TH comes up, clenched in a fist with thumb side of hand upward. 1TH then digs a hole by opening the index finger and thumb on top of 5TH.
and hid his master's money	1TH makes stuffing motion into the hole created in the other hand. Then 1TH brushes off the top of the hole and closes it. The 1TH hand that had one finger extended now has none. It is held as a fist. The 1TH fist rotates as if to look around to see where the talent has gone. Both hands disappear.
After a long time the master came	MH reappears.
and settled accounts with them.	MH makes a waving motion, beckoning the other three hands to come forward.
The servant who had received 5,000 coins came in.	5TH reappears and walks over to MH and suddenly dips down and pulls up the 2TH hand.
"You gave me 5,000 coins, sir. Look, here are another 5,000 that I have earned."	5TH and 2TH are open, palms out, fingers spread, and move side to side in a rocking motion. 2TH disappears.
"Well done, good and faithful servant," said the master.	MH gives thumbs up sign.
"You have been faithful in managing small amounts so I will put you in charge of large amounts.	MH then shakes hand with 5TH.
"Come on in and share my happiness."	MH and 5TH applaud.
Then the servant who had been given 2,000 coins came back in.	2TH appears with two fingers extended and comes over to MH.
He said, "Look, here are another 2,000 talents I've earned."	1TH appears also with two fingers extended. Both sets of fingers flash open and close. Then 1TH disappears.

THE GIVING BOOK

"Well done, you good and faithful servant," said the master.

MH makes O.K. sign by touching thumb and index finger together and extending others.

"You have been faithful in managing small amounts, so I will put you in charge of large amounts.

MH pats 2TH lightly on the back of the 2TH hand, and then the two hands shake.

"Come on in and share my happiness."

Both hands applaud.

Then the servant who had received 1,000 coins came in and said

1TH appears, making the sign of a zero by touching thumb and index finger together and having all other fingers parallel to the index finger.

"Sir, I know you are a hard master, and you reap harvest where you did not plant, and you gather crops where you did not scatter seed.

1TH immediately is extended stiff and straight, with fingers together as if it were at attention. The hand vibrates in fear.

"I was afraid, so I went off and hid your money in the ground.

1TH fingers gradually bend over, wilting in fear and drop in height so they can only be partially seen above the bottom stage line at the end of the dialogue.

"Look. Here is what belongs to you."

Fingers continue to disappear, only until 1 finger can be seen.

"You bad and lazy servant," the master said.

MH points and shakes index finger.

"You knew, did you, that I reap harvests where I did not plant and gather crops where I did not scatter seed?

MH then points fingers down at 1TH finger and moves slightly up and down.

"Well, then, you should have deposited my money in the bank and I would have received it all back with interest when I returned.

MH makes a shape of a mouth and starts moving like it is talking.

"Take the money away from him and give it to the one who has 10,000 coins.

1TH finger disappears.

"For to every person who has something, even more will be given.

MH makes a point, extending index finger and makes a sweeping motion pointing out to the whole audience.

"That person will have more than enough.

MH is turned over and opened and extended, palm out.

"But the person who has nothing,

MH is held upright, making a point with index finger extended.

"Even the little that he or she will be taken away.

Index finger of MH is held above MH's thumb, making a "C" shape and index finger and thumb gradually come together and meet.

"As for this useless servant, throw him out in darkness.

1TH reappears, making a zero.

5TH comes up and grasps wrist of useless servant and lowers 1TH hand below stage level.

"There he will cry and gnash his teeth."

1TH reappears and rubs thumb on tips of fingers, back and forth.

| Understanding II | *We hold ourselves back from using our gifts to their fullest potential.* |

Me and My Talents
(Estimated time: 20 minutes)

Distribute pencils and paper to the young people. Divide the group into smaller groups. Have them answer these questions on paper. Then they are to discuss their answers within their small groups.

1. Estimate on a scale from 1,000 to 5,000 how much ability and talent you have been given. (Make the point that everyone is given talent, and it is not important how much is given, but how wisely we use what we have been given.)
2. Estimate what percent of the above number that you actually use.
3. Name a talent of which you make good use.
4. Name a talent of which you make poor or little use.
5. Name a talent of which you would like to make better use. (Ask the students to keep the answer to this question in mind for the closing worship.)

6. How do you use a talent to the glory of God?
7. Why do you think Jesus makes the focal point of his story the person who had the least, when he usually is deeply concerned about including those people who have little?

Understanding III | *God calls us to use our gifts.*

Making the Best of What We've Been Given
(Estimated time: 20 minutes)

Have on hand an amount of money equal to at least $2.00 per person in the group. You may need to get these funds from the church budget, a willing donor, or the service or commitment committee of your church. Explain the activity by using the following paragraph.

"We have _____dollars that will be given to _____(a local needy cause) in the name of our group. This money has been given by _____. However, before we give the money away, we are going to put the parable of the talents to work. Each of you will be requested to take some of this money with you when you go tonight. You may take as little or as much as you would like, but no one is allowed to take more than _____(set your own limit). You may use this to earn more money in any way you like. You may work in groups or individually. In three weeks when we gather again you are to return the original money and any money made with it. At this time we will make the donation to _____(the local charity)."

You may wish to discuss various ideas with the young people about how they might make the best use of what they have been given.

Worship—Anointed to Give
(Estimated time: 20 minutes)

For a closing worship, use a service of anointing. Have on hand a small amount of olive oil in a bowl. Ask people to come forward and state the God-given talent or gift of which they wish to make better use. (This was question 5 in the previous discussion.) When the young people state their talent, dip the side of your thumb in the olive oil, lightly touch their forehead, and make the sign of the cross. Then using the person's name, say, "_____, I charge you to make good use of the gifts God has given you. Become all that you can be. Use your_____(talent)_____."

6

Power with Pottery

AN EXPERIENCE
TO HELP DISCOVER
THE TREASURE
HELD IN
EARTHEN VESSELS

Materials Needed

Clay—mix 1 cup salt, 1 cup flour, ½ cup water, and add food coloring. Makes enough for two or three people.

Paper to cover tables

Baking sheets

Oven

Three feet of yarn for every eight people

A candle for each person—votive candles work well

One large, free-standing candle

Matches

Copies of the opening prayer for readers

Instruments for etching in clay: toothpicks, pencils, silverware, etc.

Life is filled with metaphors. We all have experiences that, while being one thing, teach us a truth on another plane. Often the truth learned far outshines the circumstances which hold it. Christ taught with metaphors, using common elements to give parables of truth.

Throughout human experience, a truth commonly represented by metaphor is the idea that appearances can be deceiving. Things often are not as they seem. We are told not to judge a book by its cover. Others remind us that frogs are sometimes princes in disguise. Even gaining our life is to lose it. The lesson taught is that great value can be overlooked if things are taken as they appear.

Once in a children's sermon a young man offered the children two envelopes. One was neat, new, fresh, and crisp. The other, a wadded up mess, came from the bottom of a trash can. When asked to make a choice between the two, the children opted for the new envelope. After a few moments, the man revealed that the old envelope contained a five-dollar bill. The children were told to look beyond outside appearances.

Things are different from how they appear at first sight. We have seen beauty come from beasts. Treasure is found in the most unlikely places.

The Apostle Paul has taken the metaphor of appearances being deceiving one step further. He applies it to us. We, too, are not as we seem but earthen vessels holding the priceless gift. We clay pots contain the spiritual treasure of God's glory.

Could it be that we are metaphors for God? Can our collective incidences and experiences point to a greater light that outshines anything we know? Use the following activities and see.

Playing with Clay
(Estimated time: 15 minutes)

Prepare a creative play-with-clay area. As participants arrive, give them some clay. You may make it from the recipe above or purchase it. Encourage them to experiment with the clay. Provide inspirational background music to enhance their creativity. Give people the opportunity to shape and mold the clay into fun forms. Next have them design a clay pot that:

1. represents who they are,
2. tells something about them,
3. adequately holds a candle. (This is for the worship celebration. It helps to provide candles for proper sizing.)

In addition, each young person should form a clay medallion. Provide pencils, toothpicks, silverware, and other instruments for etching their initials in the medallion. The medallions do not need to be baked.

Understanding I	*We are the ones God uses to share the good news of Christ.*

Pondering People as Pottery
(Estimated time: 10 minutes)

After people complete their clay creations, sit in a circle. Have each potter share how the clay pot symbolizes who they are. Afterward, gather all the pots, place them on a cookie sheet, and bake in a slow oven (45 minutes to 1 hour at 250 degrees). Do this while the small groups share in the activities that follow.

Understanding II	*Being God's "clay pots" carries a multitude of functions and feelings.*

A Group Sculpture
(Estimated time: 20 minutes)

Form small groups of eight by first pairing up with a partner. Have the couples join with another couple. Next have the group of four join with another group of four. Group members bring their clay initials for the discussion activity that follows.

The groups of eight sit in a circle on the floor. Tie a knot in one end of a three-foot-long piece of yarn and place it in the center of the circle. This will designate the group's continuum for answering the following questions. Group members respond to the statements by placing their clay initial somewhere along the yarn line to best represent what they are feeling. Have group members discuss their responses. Use these continuum questions, and let the knotted end of the yarn line represent the first possibility and the loose end of the yarn line represent the second possibility.

1. This past week I've felt . . .
   crushed_____all together.

2. As God's creation, I feel like a . . .
   masterpiece_____back to the drawing board.

3. Lately my faith has been . . .
   I doubt it!_____no doubt about it!

Have one person read 2 Corinthians 4:7–12. Reflect on these verses in silence for a minute. Continue with the continuum.

4. As an instrument of the Lord, I feel . . .
   I've got "feet of clay"_____I'm solid as concrete.

5. Being used by God means . . .
   God keeps giving_____I keep giving.

A Group Sculpture
(Estimated time: 10 minutes)

Have each small group make a clay sculpture from the clay that was used to make everyone's initials. Form the initials into a meaningful expression of 2 Corinthians 4:7: "Yet we who have this spiritual treasure are like common clay pots, in order to show that the supreme power belongs to God, not to us." Each group selects a person to tell the larger group the meaning behind the group masterpiece. This will be done later.

Check the oven. When the pots are ready, bring them and the people together in a dimly-lit worship area. Place unlighted candles in the pots and distribute them to their owners. Use the group clay sculptures as a center altar area. Also have one large free-standing candle in the center.

Understanding III | *We celebrate God's working through us.*

THE GIVING BOOK

Worship

(Estimated time: 45 minutes)

Begin by saying, "This worship experience will explore and celebrate us as givers—the people whom God uses. It also gives us an opportunity to read, discuss, and demonstrate 2 Corinthians 3:17—4:15."

Choose three readers for the opening prayer and one person to serve as leader. The leader reads the epistle message throughout the service. The worship pattern consists of a Scripture reading, followed by an experience. It is hoped that the passage will come alive as you read and experience it more fully. Start by having the small groups tell the significance of their sculptures. Then use the following opening prayer:

LEADER: Together we begin our worship in the name of God—our Creator, Redeemer, and Holy Spirit.

READER 1: Creator God, shape us. By your imaginative, unending energy, make us special works of art, true masterpieces.

READER 2: God, our Redeemer, bring wholeness to our fragmented lives. Supply us with the hope that your forgiveness offers.

READER 3: God, O Holy Spirit, blow away the dust of discouragement, apathy, and laziness. Send your cleansing power to make us whole and holy. Amen.

LEADER: "Where the Spirit of the Lord is present, there is freedom" [2 Cor. 3:17b].

At this time, choose a favorite song of celebration. Form a circle and dance. Use motions, do a kick dance, enhance it. Celebrate the freedom the Lord brings.

Power with Pottery

LEADER: "All of us, then, reflect the glory of the Lord with uncovered faces; and that same glory, coming from the Lord, who is the Spirit, transforms us into his likeness in an ever greater degree of glory" [2 Cor. 3:18].

Light the center candle. Pass it from one person to the next. As each person receives the lighted candle, the group says, "____(name)____ reflects the glory of the Lord." When the circle is complete, place the candle in the center of the group.

LEADER: "God in his mercy has given us this work to do, and so we do not become discouraged" [2 Cor. 4:1]. One way to keep from becoming discouraged is to remember we are not alone. God has placed us together for support and encouragement. We need each other, and God uses us as special reminders. Share the "peace of the Lord" with one another. Show your support and care with a handshake or a hug.

"We put aside all secret and shameful deeds; we do not act with deceit, nor do we falsify the word of God. In the full light of truth we live in God's sight and try to commend ourselves to everyone's good conscience. For if the gospel we preach is hidden, it is hidden only from those who are being lost. They do not believe, because their minds have been kept in the dark by the evil god of this world. He keeps them from seeing the light shining on them" [2 Cor. 4:2–4a].

Please close your eyes for a time of confession. Evil thoughts and deeds keep us from seeing the light. Use this as a quiet time for personal reflection. Take a minute and make a silent confession. [Pause for a minute.]

I will say a word and then pause for a second. Use the silence for personal reflection. Anger . . . hate . . . cheating . . . gossip . . . selfishness . . . pride . . . jealousy . . . I can do anything—I don't need God . . . I can't do anything. . . .

God doesn't keep us in the dark. Our Lord let us share a magnificent hope, "the light that comes from the Good News about the glory of Christ, who is the exact likeness of God" [2 Cor. 4:4b].

Hear these words of assurance. Christ lives for us. The darkness is defeated. Live in the light, for you are forgiven! Open your eyes. Christ lives in you. "For it is not ourselves that we preach; we preach Jesus Christ as Lord, and ourselves as your servants for Jesus' sake." [2 Cor. 4:5].

Explain to the group that preaching, or proclaiming Jesus Christ, can be done through many activities. Have each group member complete this sentence: "Preaching Jesus Christ as Lord for me means . . ."

LEADER: "The God who said, 'Out of darkness the light shall shine!' is the same God who made his light shine in our hearts, to bring us the knowledge of God's glory shining in the face of Christ" [2 Cor. 4:6].

Have people hold their clay pot creations that have become candle holders. Sing "Pass It On" as the candles are lighted. Start the light around by using the one candle in the center.

LEADER: "Yet we who have this spiritual treasure are like common clay pots, in order to show that the supreme power belongs to God, not to us. We are often troubled, but not crushed; sometimes in doubt, but never in despair; there are many enemies, but we are never without a friend; and though badly hurt at times, we are not destroyed. At all times we carry in our mortal bodies the death of Jesus, so that his life also may be seen in our bodies. Throughout our lives we are always in danger of death for Jesus' sake, in order that his life may be seen in this mortal body of ours. This means that death is at work in us, but life is at work in you" [2 Cor. 4:7–12].

Encourage participants to share personal experiences that reflect on their lives as "clay pots." Then talk about what it means to be an instrument of God.

LEADER: "The Scripture says, 'I spoke because I believed.' In the same spirit of faith we also speak because we believe" [2 Cor. 4:13].

The group stands, join hands, and recites the Apostles' Creed (see below). Begin in a whisper, and gradually get louder. At the same time you are speaking the creed, raise your joined hands slowly. The "Amen" should be a triumphant affirmation of your faith.

Let people keep their candles and clay pots as a reminder that we are all givers, God's special people with a special purpose.

THE APOSTLES' CREED

I believe in God the Father Almighty, Maker of heaven and earth;

And in Jesus Christ His only Son our Lord; who was conceived by the Holy Ghost, born of the Virgin Mary, suffered under Pontius Pilate, was crucified, dead, and buried; He descended into hell; the third day He rose again from the dead; He ascended into heaven, and sitteth on the right hand of God the Father Almighty; from thence He shall come to judge the quick and the dead.

I believe in the Holy Ghost; the holy Catholic Church; the communion of saints; the forgiveness of sins; the resurrection of the body; and the life everlasting. Amen.

7

Being a Star, or the Gift of Success

AN INVITATION TO
BECOME A "STAR"
AND SHINE WITH
GOD'S INTENDED
LIGHT

Materials Needed

"Sky's the Limit Box," with
scissors, glue, crayons,
markers, gummed stars,
glitter, foil, newsprint,
construction paper,
Starburst Candy, babyfood
jars, yarn (including one big
ball for every five people),
writing paper and masking
tape

Bibles

Pencils

Milky Way bars, chocolate
stars, Twinkies, Rice Krispie
star bars, or star-shaped
cookies

Our human nature automatically assumes the "me-view" of success. Whatever I do is done in order to prove myself. My need is to impress others so I look good. I am constantly measuring my worth by comparing myself with somebody else. By putting others down, I profess to be on the top. Climbing the "ladder of success" is a selfish endeavor. Most of all, the "me-view" is seeing myself all alone and on my own.

The "me-view" soon leads to the frustrating and futile result of never quite making it. When left entirely up to me, being a success can be a desperate, lonely, empty struggle.

From our Lord's perspective, the world's standards for success are turned upside down. The "me-view" becomes the "we-view." In baptism I am connected with the Lord of Life. My value and worth is seen in light of Christ. I am no longer a "me" but a "we." The "we-view" replaces the desperate struggle to be in control with the challenging dynamics of a team. Whatever I do is God using me, working in me, shining through me.

Being joined with Christ also means being joined with one another. Together, we are Christ's body, Christ's people, Christ's church. Instead of comparing my talents and gifts with others, I can freely celebrate each person's uniqueness. Our adventure is to become the best persons we can be. By using Jesus as our example, we can see success in the light of a servant lifestyle. The paradox is that in the serving we truly shine as stars—lights of the world. What freedom to be able to shine as servant-stars!

Comparison is transformed from an activity between people into an opportunity for knowing one's potential. Growth and success are measured by how far I have come in my personal journey and how I have grown in relationship with God. I must see myself as a star—chosen by God to shine wherever I am. Who I am is who God is shining through me. What I do is what God is doing as God uses me.

Before the group arrives, prepare an *atmosphere of "stars."* The atmosphere can be as simple or elaborate as you wish. Twinkling Christmas star lights to plug in or construction paper stars hung from the ceiling add sparkle. Decorations create the mood of being and seeing ourselves as God's stars.

Make a giant newsprint banner with the words, "YOU MUST SHINE AMONG THEM LIKE STARS . . ." (Phil. 2:15*b*). Leave an empty space on the banner for attaching star tags later in the worship celebration.

Getting Started

Name Tags
(Estimated time: 15 minutes)

Have the young people design five-point star tags from construction paper, and write their name in the center. On each of the star's points, let everyone complete the sentence: "When I'm successful, I feel . . ." There will be five different answers, one on each point. Use yarn to make the star into a pendant to wear. (You'll need the star tags for later, so make sure everyone keeps them throughout the evening.)

When everyone has completed their star tags, gather the group and share the theme of the evening by saying, "We are here to celebrate success and discover the stars we are." Have each person share his or her name and the answers on the star tags. Pray, asking for God's blessing on your learning and discoveries.

| *Understanding I* | We need to discover and affirm personal success and the success of others. |

Star Sculpture

(Estimated time: 10 minutes)

Form a circle. Instead of numbering "one, two, one, two," whisper the word "twinkle" to the first person. Whisper the word "shine" to the second person. Continue around the circle, whispering "twinkle" and "shine" until everyone has a word. To form two groups, have people close their eyes and say their word. The object is to find those with the same word.

Once the two groups have gathered, they are ready to play "Star Sculpture." The leader calls out what both groups are to form. By using all members, the groups are to interpret/create/build a human sculpture as quickly as possible. Have the groups make sculptures as a star, the big dipper, the little dipper, or representing success, or shining. Make up some of your own possibilities!

Spin a Yarn

(Estimated time: 15 minutes)

Divide into new groups of five to make yarn stars. Members of each group sit knee to knee in a circle. Begin with one person holding a ball of yarn and answering the incomplete sentence. The person then holds the end of the yarn, and tosses the ball to someone across from the circle. The person receiving the ball completes the same sentence, holds onto the yarn, and tosses the ball to someone else. The group gradually forms a star design with the yarn. When the ball returns to the original person, begin again with a new sentence starter. For a fun finishing touch, secure the star points with masking tape. As a group, attach the star somewhere in the room.

Here are some suggested sentence starters:
   * A star is someone who . . .
   * To me, being unsuccessful means . . .
   * A time when I really shined at school was . . .
   * In my family, I'm a star when . . .
   * I view myself as successful with my friends when . . .
   * Jesus was successful/unsuccessful because . . .

Taking a Stand on Success
(Estimated time: 15 minutes)

As an opportunity for the entire group to voice ideas, draw an imaginary line in the room. Designate where the line ends and begins, for this is where people will "take a stand" as they answer questions. There are two choices, so people will stand at one end of the line or the other. Encourage them to share the "whys" of their opinions. Here are some either-or questions to select from. Feel free to add your own:

— Whose success is most difficult to handle: your own or someone else's?

— What does success give you: a big head or a big heart?

— What do you fear most: success or failure?

— How would you describe a successful person: the servant or the one to be served?

— Do you think God wants us to be a success: yes or no?

— Do you view yourself as a success: yes or no?

Understanding II | *We often struggle with our perspective of success.*

Shining and Falling Stars
(Estimated time: 15 minutes)

Try this as a way to "chews" new groups: Starburst Candy comes in five colors. Color candy-code small groups by counting out enough candy for everyone. For example, to get five groups in a group of fifteen, hand out three green, three yellow, three orange, three red, three pink. Hand each person a Starburst Candy. Form groups by matching candy colors.

After people are in small groups (eight or less), distribute Bibles and Bible verses. Scripture references could be written on slips of paper ahead of time and sealed with gummed stars.

The Bible is filled with "star" stories. Some are "success" examples of God using people to shine as they live out their relationships. Other stories reveal "falling" stars—those who lost sight of whose they are. Read some of the following Bible stories and be ready to

* tell the story or example,
* define whether it is the "me-view" or "we-view" of success (see introduction),
* share the result of that view.

Genesis 11:1–9 (Tower of Babel)

Genesis 22:1–14 (Abraham and Isaac)

Judges 4:17–22 (Deborah and Jael)

Judges 7:1–21 (Gideon)

1 Samuel 18:6–16 (Saul and David)

Matthew 5:1–12 (Beatitudes)

Matthew 20:1–16 (Workers in the vineyard)

Luke 2:36–38 (Anna)

Luke 10:38–42 (Mary and Martha)

Luke 18:9–14 (Pharisee and the publican)

John 4:7–29 (Woman at the well)

John 13:3–17 (Jesus washing the disciples' feet)

Acts 5:1–5 (Ananais and Sapphira)

Share your discoveries.

Star Jars
(Estimated time: 20 minutes)

To affirm one another as stars and prepare for the worship celebration, form pairs. Have people make "star jars" for their partners. Encourage the young people to be as creative as they can and to be sure that the jar has their partner's name on it. Use empty baby food jars and whatever else from the "Sky's the Limit" box. Set a five-to-seven-minute time limit for this project.

Distribute slips of paper so each person has enough slips for every other person in the group. (If your group has more than twelve people, divide into the earlier yarn-star groups of five for this activity.)

On each slip of paper, have people write, "_____(name)_____, you are a star to me because. . ." Complete the statement with a positive comment, fold, and seal with a gummed star. Have people write a statement for each person in the group. Fill the jars with good words to take home.

| Understanding III | As God's people, we can continually celebrate our success in the light of Christ! |

Shining and Sharing

(Estimated time: 15 minutes)

Gather the group in a circle with the warmth of candlelight as a reminder of our Lord's love, and sit near the "yet-to-be-completed" banner. Join in singing some favorite songs, including Epiphany songs, songs of light and love.

Epiphany is a time for sharing and shining. Stars do that well. All people are stars that continually need to be reminded of God's point of view. Whether it is in success or failure, we are not alone. We are joined with the God of light, the Great Giver, and Forgiver.

Just as God used an Epiphany star to point others to the Christ child, God uses us today. We are the stars used to point others to Jesus Christ. What a privilege to claim!

Read Philippians 2:13–16a to the group: ". . . God is always at work in you to make you willing and able to obey his own purpose. Do everything without complaining or arguing, so that you may be innocent and pure as God's perfect children, who live in a world of corrupt and sinful people. You must shine among them like stars lighting up the sky, as you offer them the message of life."

Next sing a song that can be personalized. "Jesus in the Morning" works well. For each verse, replace the name of Jesus with each person's name. While the group sings the name of the person in the verse, that person attaches his or her star tag to complete the banner. When all the participants have added their star tags, it becomes a "star-spangled banner"!

Read 2 Corinthians 4:6 to the group: "The God who said, 'Out of darkness the light shall shine!' is the same God who made his light shine in our hearts, to bring us the knowledge of God's glory shining in the face of Christ."

Invite participants to share what this passage means in their lives. As a benediction, join hands and have each person say a blessing and prayer of thanks for the star on her or his right.

Top off the evening with surprise "star" treats! How about Milky Way candy bars? Chocolate stars or Twinkies? Maybe Rice Krispie star bars or star-shaped cookies? Use your imagination—you, too, are a star!

8

Gifts from the One Who Makes the Shadows Dance

A SERIES OF
ACTIVITIES
TO DISCOVER
AND EXPLORE
GOD'S PRESENCE
WITH US

Materials Needed
Bibles
Clay to make wind chimes
Rolling pins
Kitchen utensils
Clear nylon fishing wire
Sticks or wood for cross pieces
Wood blocks, strips of metal,
  tubing, or bamboo pieces
Something to drill holes
Balloons
Straws
Water-based tempera paint
Heavy stock paper
Bubble mix
Record with wind sounds

Everyone knows that leaves have different shapes. From the friendly hand-shaped sassafras to the pointed symmetrical maple, each has its own character. Far more difficult to perceive is that, like leaves, trees have identifiable shapes. The silhouette of a pine offers a striking contrast to the shadows of a live oak. Individual trees have their own uniquely constructed forms. What creates their architecture? Sometimes animals eat or break the limbs. Neighboring trees will cause other trees to stretch or spread to gain sunlight. Like all of us, trees go through years of plenty and want that encourage or deny growth.

Perhaps the most influential force that gives a tree its definition is the unseen hand of the wind. An experienced forest watcher can glance at a stand of trees and tell the predominant wind direction. Trees close to the seashore will sometimes look lopsided, their stature etched by the single direction of incoming sea breezes. A tornado can completely take away a tree's shape, leaving only a stump where a work of art once stood.

Despite its power and influence, the wind remains unseen. We may feel it, hear it, see its results, but the wind lies beyond the grasp of our knowing. This one that makes the shadows dance exists beyond our control.

What forces exert their pressure and extend their touch to give us our unique shapes? Certainly mentors and friends have influenced our growth. The same may be said of where we extend our roots. But what wind brings friends together or blows us to a particular place? Our life-shape comes from the unseen presence of God's wind. The Holy Spirit, God's presence with us, is referred to in Scripture as wind, or breath. The wind refreshes, pushes, shapes, and directs. Breath offers life. Yet both are unseen, illusive, and out of our control. We know breath and wind are present but largely through their wonderful and mighty results.

The next chapter is designed so that you may find and know the wind of God. Listen and you may hear quiet breezes or a mighty roar. The movement is ours to behold.

Spirited Sharing
(Estimated time: 10 minutes)

After the group has arrived, designate the four corners of the room as corner one, corner two, corner three, and corner four. Tell the young people you will be naming four kinds of air or wind that the Holy Spirit might be like for them. Each will correspond to one of the corners of the room. They are to listen to the four possibilities and decide what kind of wind or air they think best describes the Spirit for them. Then they are to go and stand in that particular corner.

Use the following descriptions.

The Spirit for you is more like . . .

	1	2	3	4
A.	Sea breeze	Toronado	Wind from a ceiling fan	Someone whistling
B.	Air from a furnace	A March wind	Blowing out birthday candles	Being out of breath
C.	Cool breeze in summer	Breath from a person	A blizzard wind	Air coming out of a balloon

People who gather in the specific corners share with each other why they feel the way they do about the Spirit. Then a spokesperson for each small group tells the others in the room some of the responses made in his or her group. The whole process is to be done three times, using a different set of winds or air each time.

Understanding I | *The Holy Spirit is God's presence with us.*

Catching Your Breath

(Estimated time: 10 minutes)

When the opening activity has been completed, explain that the fellowship activity time will be spent discovering how God is present with us as the Holy Spirit.

Break the group into smaller groups and have them read the description of the Holy Spirit found in Romans 8:9–27. Let groups come up with as many characteristics describing the Holy Spirit and its activity as possible.

Explain that the Greek and Hebrew words sometimes used for spirit also mean wind and breath. When we read, we use certain punctuation marks to know where to breathe and make a sentence's meaning clear. Ask individuals to apply this to the Spirit and decide whether the Spirit in the passage is more like

- **.** a period—finality
- **!** an exclamation point—great impact
- **?** a question mark—wondering
- **,** a comma—pause, or waiting
- **. . .** dot, dot, dot—to be continued

Ask which of these marks would express the breath of the Spirit in their own lives. These responses may be first written and then shared, or simply discussed.

Understanding II	*The Holy Spirit is unpredictable, not under our control, and cannot be seen or defined.*

The Wonder of Wind

(Estimated time: 40 minutes)

Let the groups read the story of Nicodemus found in John 3:1–12. Focus on verse 8. Encourage the group to discover what this says about God and God's presence with us in the Holy Spirit.

For an activity to remind the group of God's remarkable changing, free presence make wind chimes. These can be made out of potter's clay if you have access to a kiln, or if a ceramic shop is near. Use a rolling pin to roll clay out into a uniform thickness, approximately ¼" thick. Cut the clay into long rectangles, roughly 6" to 11" long, and 1" to 2½" wide. Put a hole in the top of each strip, though not too close to the edge. This will be used for string to

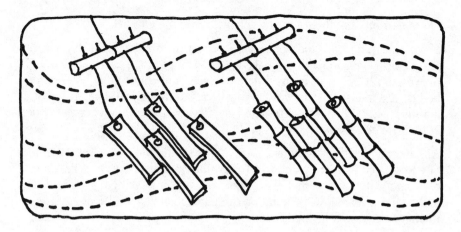

hang the chime later. Use kitchen utensils to make designs on the chimes if you like.

After the chimes have been bisque fired, use 10-pound-test clear nylon fishing wire to hang them. A stick or drift wood can be used as a cross piece above on which to tie your chimes. If you have the time and inclination before preparing the chimes to hang, you might wish to glaze them and have them fired a second time. Glazing will give them color and offer protection against breakage.

Wood blocks, strips of metal, tubing, or pieces of bamboo are inexpensive and can be used in place of clay if you like. You will need to have holes drilled through the material so the chimes can be hung. Make your chimes varying lengths so that the different sounds will be achieved.

Talk with the group about what kind of melody or song the Spirit of God is singing in and around their lives.

Understanding III | *The Holy Spirit can't be seen, but the results of the Holy Spirit can.*

Results of the Spirit

(Estimated time: 25 minutes)

Begin this next activity by pointing out that the Holy Spirit, like the wind or air sometimes used to describe it, cannot be seen, but the results may be known. Ask the group if they can point to ways the Holy Spirit has acted in their lives. See if anyone was aware of this at the time the activity or relationship occurred.

Gifts from the One Who Makes the Shadows Dance

Do one or more of the following activities with the group.

For a celebration of God's presence in our lives made known through the Holy Spirit, have individuals make balloon sculptures. This can be done by blowing up balloons of many different shapes and colors. The balloons can be tied together with string, taped together, put in a plastic bag, attached to a wall, pole, or whatever. They can be whimiscal or somehow representative of their experience.

Another good activity is straw painting. Put small amounts of several colors of water-based tempera paint on a heavy stock paper. Take straws, flatten one end, and cut them so that they taper into a point. With the tapered end toward the paint, blow the paint on the paper, creating a work of art. Experiment and see what happens.

Still another fun activity would be to blow bubbles. Make the bubble mix as follows (makes enough for two or three people): 1 tablespoon dish detergent, 2 tablespoons water, 4 drops corn syrup. For giant bubbles, add 1 teaspoon glycerine and a pinch of sugar. Glycerine is inexpensive and sold at drug stores. For colored bubbles, simply add food coloring. Then use food graters, coat hangers, fruit jar rings, wire whisks, rubber bands, slotted spoons, 6-pack holders, embroidery hoops, shaped wire, or whatever to create your bubbles. See how big, how small, how many different kinds of bubbles the group can create.

Wind in Worship
(Estimated time: 10 minutes)

For worship, have the sound of the wind blowing in the background. If mother nature will not cooperate, most record stores have records with recorded sounds of the wind that you may purchase. Gather everyone together and invite them to a brief period of silence to listen to the sound of the wind. Do so by saying:

"Let us be silent for a moment so that we might listen to the sounds of the wind. Listen. What wind blows across your days?"

Silence.

"A wind pushing us to a new place?"

Silence.

"We can do all things through Christ, who strengthens us" [Phil. 4:13].

Silence.

"A cool breeze in the heat of summer?"

Silence.

"Give thanks to God, for God is good."

Silence.

"A dry, but stifled breeze?"

Silence.

"Behold, God is making all things new" [cf. Rev. 21:5].

Silence.

"A wind that makes kites fly and shadows dance?"

Silence.

"Give thanks to God, for God is good."

Silence.

"A roaring storm that overwhelms us?"

Silence.

"And Christ came to them upon the waters and stilled the storm" [cf. Mark 6:45–51].

Silence.

"A wind with spring on its breath, blowing our winter away?"

Silence.

"Give thanks to God, for God is good."

Encourage the group to think about concerns that they have and to summarize them in one or two words to be used in a prayer. Begin the prayer by having two readers use these preparatory sentences.

READER 1: Only the grace of God enables us to make sense of life.

READER 2: The wind blows where it wills.

READER 1: You know not whither it comes or where it goes.

READER 2: The Spirit intercedes for us with sighs too deep for words.

READER 1: Let us pray, offering our words of concern.

Close by singing songs that deal with wind, breath, or the Holy Spirit. Possibilities include "Blowin' in the Wind," "Where Does the Wind Blow," "Breathe on Me, Breath of God," or "Spirit of God, Descend upon My Heart."

9

The Gifts That Make Life Abundant

ACTIVITIES
TO DISCOVER
THE ABUNDANCE
OF LIFE

Materials Needed
Small paper sack for each
 person
"Punch hole" camera for each
 person
Pencils
Paper
Bibles (John 10:1–10)

Two graduating high school seniors were discussing the future. Amid all the hoopla of parties, senior day, annuals, and proms, some very basic questions awaited answers. The talk centered on what one girl was going to do when she got her diploma. Going to college came next, but she really wasn't sure what she wanted from life. The girl observed, "It seems sometimes that we are born to go to school, go to college, get a job, work, and then die. It's too much to get excited about." The friend then quipped, "But it's the elaborations that make it interesting!"

At its basic level, life is going from a beginning to an end. As Christians we can be grateful for the elaborations that make our days more than a connecting of the dots of birth and death in the shortest possible way. We are spared this outlook through Jesus Christ, the ultimate elaboration of God's love. Once we discover what God is like through Jesus, we have a new outlook. Worries and fear can never hold the same sway. The security and safety given in grace enable us to see more clearly, appreciate more deeply, and love more fully.

Auntie Mame said something to the effect that all life's a banquet but most poor souls are starving to death. God responds through Christ and says, "I came that they may have life, and have it abundantly" (John 10:10*b*, RSV). Shining eyes. Mile-high meringue pies. The book of Ecclesiastes. Popcorn and movies. Letters and cross-country Christmas cards. Grey sweaters. Old photographs and their power to induce immediate wistfulness. James Michener. Willie Nelson. Southern mannerisms. The sound of a canoe paddle in the water. The familiar feel of a loved one's hand. Clam chowder. Summer's lazy sound of a distant lawn mower. Joke-telling friends. Mexican mariachis. Almanacs. Slender glass buildings. Thank God for all the elaborations that give life its vast richness.

Read on to become more aware of the elaborations that lift life and of the one life which makes it so.

The Object Is Discovery
(Estimated time: 20 minutes)

As the group arrives, give each person a small paper sack and tell them that the group will begin by playing "Seek and Hide." Explain that they are to go throughout the church (outdoors can be included if you wish) and find an object that will fit in the sack. Others will try to guess the object's identity by reaching inside the sack and touching the object but not seeing it. When the group returns with their objects, have one person take her sack around to all the other people so that they can try to guess the object. All wait to share their guesses until everyone has had a chance to put their hand inside the sack.

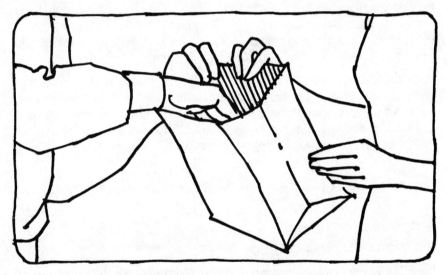

Explain that the activities in today's time together are to open us to seeing life and each other in new ways. Point out how much of life can be taken for granted and that often we miss the abundant life God intends for us.

| *Understanding I* | *By taking God's gifts for granted, we miss the abundant life that can be ours.* |

Focus on Things

(Estimated time: 15 minutes)

Have "punch hole cameras" ready for this activity or let the young people make them. The "cameras" are made by punching a single hole in an index card or in the center of a sheet of paper. Tell the group that they are to again explore the meeting area by taking "pictures" with their "cameras." Distribute pencils and paper and ask young people to record ten things that they are able to see in a new way with their cameras. Point out that the vision can be enlarged by holding the camera close or made smaller by holding the camera farther away. Set a time limit. When the group returns, have people share one of the ten things they saw.

Focus on Us

(Estimated time: 20 minutes)

Explain that you will now be shifting the focus to each other and that not only do we take objects for granted but also people. Tell the group that you would like them not to take each other for granted but to be able to see each other in new and abundant ways. Ask the group, "What would you like to know about each other that you don't already know?"

Have them suggest questions to be asked. Record the suggestions on a flip-chart or chalkboard. You may not be able to do all of them due to time limitations. Agree upon the questions to be asked and go through them, one at a time, giving everyone a chance to answer. To conclude the discussion, ask the group to share what things they learned that surprised them.

Understanding II | *God gives us the gift of abundant life.*

Scripture Study

(Estimated time: 15 minutes)

Have the group divide into smaller groups and read John 10:1–10. Encourage them to write responses to the following open-ended statements:

1. The "thief" that comes to destroy abundant life for me is . . .
2. A way that I am given abundant life through Christ is . . .
3. I am most aware of having abundant life when . . .
4. I lost sight of abundant life when . . .

Discuss the responses in small groups.

Right Now I Am . . .

(Estimated Time: 15 minutes)

Begin the next activity by saying, "Jesus Christ has come, setting us free to fully experience the world and each other. Often we lose this sense of freedom with each other and meet only on the most surface of levels. As a way to break through our surfaces and discover the abundance of each other, we are going to complete the statement, 'Right now I am . . . ' seven times."

Go through this either in pairs or with one individual responding while the whole group listens. Encourage participants to take risks in sharing themselves. The first responses may be safe and mundane, like "Right now I am tired" or "Right now I am feeling silly" or "Now I am hungry." As the exercise progresses, responses ideally will become more significant, like "Right now I am struggling with my family" or "Now I am lonely." Don't be afraid to follow the conversations that could result.

| *Understanding III* | *We are to give thanks for the gifts of God which make life abundant.* |

Thanksgiving and Thanksliving

(Estimated time: 15 minutes)

Ask individuals to write the name of a person, place, thing, skill or gift, event or activity which lifts their lives and makes them abundant. Share these and why they are special with each other.

For worship, ask people to pick one of the above sources of abundance. Pray, giving God thanks for the abundance and vast richness of life. Let the participants share their sources in a word or two. Conclude the prayer with everyone singing, "Amen." Close the session by singing the "Doxology."

10

Out of the Ordinary Gifts

In the twelfth chapter of John, a voice comes from heaven while Jesus teaches. For the moment, Jesus loses the crowd's attention. They debate. Did they hear thunder? Or was it an angel speaking? No consensus is reached, and Jesus resumes teaching. The debate continues today as we seek the movement of God across our lives. Was it a chance thing or a God thing? Was it an angel or thunder?

When given the opportunity, we find it easier to hear thunder. It is just the sound of the typewriter in the next room. Never mind the hands that move so intricately above the keys. It is just the sound of kids playing in the yard. You have heard it a thousand times before, and it is only chance that you listen again. It is just the sound of an old friend's voice. Surely it was only chance that brought you two to the same restaurant. You do the ordinary thing and talk about the paths your lives have taken. You think of how you have made it and how you have not. It is only a coincidence that you re-examine your life, the friend's face serving as a reminder. Is it only thunder? It certainly rumbles inside.

However, if you and I will pause and listen, if we will hear with more than our ears, we will discover that the sounds of our days have meaning. They call with a subtleness, and if we are quick to listen, we can hear the angels speaking. As Frederick Buechner says in *The Sacred Journey*, "The question is not whether the things that happen to you are chance things or God's things because, of course, they are both at once. There is no chance thing through which God cannot speak."

God uses the chance things in life, but why? God loves and values all creation. If nothing is left to chance, then think of the esteem in which God holds the world. The most ordinary things can become holy. Bread—flour from wheat and water—becomes God's body. Wine—the juice of grapes—becomes Christ's life blood. And they are here, or God is here, in our midst. The common can be celebrated because God is in it speaking to us, touching our memories with the smell of honeysuckle, healing our hurts with a walk through the neighborhood.

But more than things have value. If God speaks to us through the chance things of life, imagine the way *we* are valued! Every little off-hand remark, each trite phrase, has the potential to be more than a rumble echoing in the air. God holds us in such high esteem that God can speak through us to heal hearts, burn bridges, and dry tears. God loves us enough to be in us, making our words more than just our words. Everything we say and do can be used to touch a being, to influence a life, or to fill a hollow.

Mrs. Dobbins was a crusty old English teacher—at least that is how she seemed to a fifteen-year-old. I suspect that if I knew her now, I would see her differently. I would understand that some of her crustiness came from a heart having to bear the hurt of a husband lost too early in life. Despite her crustiness, Mrs. Dobbins has stayed with me. The one thing she did for me was to teach me the beauty and power of words. To this day she does not know the impact she had on my life: my love of reading words, my wanting to write words, my needing to say the right word, and finally, my wanting to give people the Word made flesh. She probably does not remember those influential phrases offered in some obscure class, but I can never forget them. Somehow, in her voice, I heard the angel speaking.

This chapter seeks to assist you in discovering gifts that come from the ordinary fabric of life. If even for a moment young people hear the rustle of angel wings in the simple and subtle, then the effort will be worth it. What greater gift can be given than the ability to discern God?

A SENIOR HIGH EVENT
DISCOVERING
GIFTS THAT COME
OUT OF THE
ORDINARY

Materials Needed

Ten to fifteen poster boards

Pens for drawing on the poster boards

Paper for everyone

Pencils for everyone

Several high-intensity reading lamps

One cassette recorder for every seven people

One cassette tape for every seven people

Two pieces of construction paper

Masking tape

An "Art Gallery" Visit
(Estimated time: 15 minutes)

To begin this activity, set up an "art gallery." Take a piece of poster board and copy a simple design. It should not look like anything in particular but could appear to be several things. You want a simple drawing that different people will see in different ways. You may use the samples below. These come from Bannerman and Fakkema's *Guide for Recreational Leaders* (p. 18). Once the first drawing is completed, do several more until you have ten to fifteen "works of art." Display them in the room where the group is to meet. Bring several high intensity reading lamps from home. Use these to project added light on your "works of art." This will heighten the effect and create the feel of a gallery.

Give young people pencils and paper as they arrive. Have them write what they think each drawing is. Ask them not to share their responses with anyone for now since they will be doing that later. Let people mill around the room and look at the drawings. When all have arrived and had an opportunity to identify the "works of art," bring the group together. Go through the pictures one by one and let the group share what they saw. Hold one picture at a time and have people call out what they think it is. Have individuals give reasons for the identifications they have made. The object is not to come

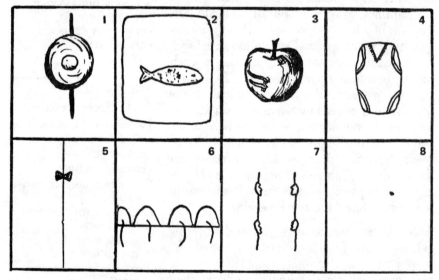

1. A bird's eye view of a Mexican boy riding a bicycle.
2. A rich sardine in its private can.
3. A worm taking a date to dinner.
4. A people neck sweater for turtles.
5. A man with a bow tie caught in an elevator door.
6. The rear view of a rat race about to start.
7. A bear climbing a tree.
8. A ghost with a cinder in its eye.

THE GIVING BOOK

up with a right or wrong answer but to point out that people can see the same things and have very different ideas as to what they see.

Introduce the session by saying, "Today we are going to look at some of the ordinary parts of life and discover if we can see anything extraordinary about them." Point out that in the previous activity the group took what appeared to be meaningless drawings and found meaning in them.

| Understanding I | The ordinary parts of life have value if we are open to discovering them. |

Soundings

(Estimated time: 40 minutes)

To prepare for the next activity, you will need to have a cassette recorder and a cassette tape for at least every seven persons. Before hand, prerecord each cassette tape with four easily-recognizable sounds. The sounds could include a telephone ringing, a door opening, a car starting, a typist typing, a radio broadcasting, a dog barking, a bit of conversation, a shower curtain being closed and water starting, bacon frying, or whatever. Let your imagination guide you. Use one particular sound as one of the four sounds on all of the tapes.

Divide the large group into smaller groups of no more than seven people and no fewer than four people. Give each a recorder and a cassette. Tell them that their cassette contains a recording of four sounds. Explain that they are to create a brief drama using the four sounds they have been given. After allowing the groups sufficient time to "get their act together," have them present their plays for one another.

Following the dramas, briefly discuss how the sounds were used. Talk about how the groups gave meaning to random sounds. Two helpful questions might be:

1. Was the sound that each group had in common used in different ways? If so, what were the ways? For example, a door opening could be the entrance of a hero or a villian, or pushed open by the wind. It could be a fearful, exciting, or ordinary experience.

2. What other ways had you thought about using the sounds you were given?

| Understanding II | God is known in the ordinary. |

Thunder or Angel?
(Estimated time: 20 minutes)

Before the next activity, write the word "thunder" on one piece of construction paper. On another piece, write the word "angel." Tape the papers on opposite walls or on one wall about fifteen feet apart from one another.

Have someone read John 12:20–33. Afterward, explain how we can hear God in many different voices and in many different ways. Gather the group between the two signs. Tell them that you are going to call out a situation. They are to decide quickly whether for them it is thunder or an angel speaking. As soon as they have decided, they are to go and stand under the sign that represents their choice. Remind people that they are to use their own actual experiences.

Once the group has settled under their choices, have individuals share their particular situations and why it was thunder or an angel speaking to them. Listen nonjudgmentally. Remember the activity's purpose is not to determine the correctness of the choices but to encourage sharing and to allow young people to affirm their own values. Appropriate responses from the leader might include, "so for you, arguing with your parents was thunder." Or, "tell me why that was an angel speaking?" It is important that the young people speak to the leader and not debate each other's responses.

Situations that can be used include:
1. A recent conversation with your parents
2. Something you remember a minister or teacher saying
3. Something that happened in school
4. Something your best friend said
5. A particular moment with your youth group
6. A meal you remember
7. A trip
8. An argument

Try this enjoyable variation of the activity. After the group has finished responding to one of the situations, they are to think of another situation in which they heard the opposite of their first choice. For example, the leader would say, "Now I would like you to think of another conversation with your parents when you had the opposite reaction. When you've thought of a new conversation, those of you under the thunder sign move to the angel sign, and those under the angel sign move to the thunder sign." Have the group share their responses again.

It is helpful to divide people into two groups if there are twenty or more participants. Let one group respond to half of the situations while the other listens. Then change places. One last thing: the best sharing is that which is encouraged but not required.

Understanding III | *If we look, we shall see God in ourselves.*

Significance from the Ordinary
(Estimated time: 15 minutes)

Give everyone pencils and paper. Have people pair up with someone they know and sit back-to-back. The leader then says, "without peeking, write what you remember about your partner's eye color, if their shoes tie, if they have on any jewelry, and what it looks like, if they're wearing a watch, and the number of buttons on their shirt." The pairs share their results.

Next, have the pairs sit knee-to-knee. The leader instructs them by saying, "I would like you to remember a time that was significant to you with this person, or with the youth group, or a time in church. After you have thought of the incident, share it with your partner."

Allow some time to pass. Continue, "Now I would like each of you to look underneath and through the incident you remembered, and try to see how God used that ordinary time. Also, tell your partner how the particular time changed you." After sharing is completed, encourage the pairs to tell each other of a time when they were thunder to someone and of another time when they were an angel speaking.

An Extraordinary Celebration
(Estimated time: 20 minutes)

Begin closing worship by singing favorite songs. Let people share a particular memory they have with a song and why it is important.

If your tradition allows you to celebrate the Lord's Supper or to have an agape feast, do so. Focus on how ordinary bread and wine take on extraordinary meaning. The same can be done with baptism, placing the focus on how ordinary water sets us apart to do extraordinary things and be extraordinary people. Lead the group through a renewal of their baptismal vows.

Close with a prayer, thanking God for things which are taken for granted. Let individuals in the group offer one-word prayers, mentioning people, times, or things which are ordinary but have special meaning for them.

11

The Gift That Fits like a Glove

For years left-handed people have suffered in silence. They feel like social misfits trying to use a butter knife. Left-handers remember hanging their arms off the little right-handed desks in high school. Even a screw driver is a right-handed tool. Many left-handed people who use Polaroid cameras have interesting collections of photos of their wrist, taken when they reach around with their left hand to snap the picture. Every left-handed person has heard someone say, "It's a right-handed world, and you'd better get used to it." The message is clear: deny our individual needs and conform to the expected way.

All of us have felt like Jack Nicholson in *Five Easy Pieces* when he wanted an order of toast. The waitress told him that the restaurant had no toast. Nicholson said, "What do you mean? Do you have bread?" The woman said, "Yes, we have bread, but there's no toast on the menu." She was absolutely inflexible. In exasperation, Nicholson replied: "Give me a chicken-salad sandwich on toasted white bread and hold the chicken salad!"

As Christians we live in a world that seems at best indifferent to our needs. We gather because of a God who strikes at the very heart of what robs us of our humanity. God cares enough about us to know us as individuals. God's love is molded to fit our needs. We respond in faith to a God who, instead of saying, "Come and conform to my ways," said, "I will come to you."

The two passages explored in this chapter offer shining examples of Christ coming to us and conforming his love to our particular situation. What a remarkable contrast they give to our all-too-typical experiences. A deaf man is taken from a shouting crowd. Christ knows the isolation in his envelope of silence. Then he does things that seem to be very strange. Christ puts his fingers in the man's ears and then touches his tongue.

Next Jesus looks skyward. These are odd actions to those of us who hear. Yet Jesus is actually telling the man in sign language what he is going to do. He will open his ears, heal his tongue, and the help will come from heaven. Jesus shapes his actions so that they meet the man's individual situation. Another little man is in a tree trying to get a glance, trying to get a chance to know Christ. Jesus seeks Zacchaeus out where he is and says, "Zacchaeus, make haste and come down; for I must stay at your house today" (Luke 19:5, RSV). Once again the Lord meets the need of someone where he happens to be.

Always Jesus reaches lovingly to us in a way we will understand. Our location or the particulars of our situation never stop God from loving us. We are connected to One who sees us as unique individuals and meets our needs accordingly. The Lord of grace is always striving to feed our hungers and respond to our concerns. God sees us not as a group of people but as persons. To our Maker, we are each known as having a unique set of hopes and hurts, dreams and drudgeries. God loves us with a love that is tailor-made to fit the contours of our hearts.

This chapter reminds us again that God knows our individual needs and loves us accordingly.

AN ACTIVITY REMINDING US OF THE GIFT THAT FITS LIKE A GLOVE

Materials Needed
Construction paper
Scissors for each group
Staples for each group
Stapler(s) for each group
Box (to collect gloves)
Bibles (to read Scripture)
Several old ties
Combs
Several old large man's shirts
Cereal or English peas
Utensils to eat food
Juice
Cups

Understanding I | *We have greater potential when our needs are recognized and met.*

A "Glovely" Activity
(Estimated time: 10 minutes)

In preparation for the first activity, have each person bring a pair of gloves from home. Many kinds of gloves can be used—garden gloves, golf gloves, surgical gloves, handbell gloves, mittens, rubber gloves, racquetball gloves, leather gloves, and even ski gloves although they may be somewhat difficult. You will also need construction paper, scissors, staples, and a stapler.

Getting Started

When people arrive, collect their gloves. Place the assortment of gloves in a box. After all are present, pass the box around the room and have each person pick two gloves. The gloves chosen do not have to be mates, but no one is allowed to choose the pair they brought with them. Then lead the group into the activity by saying, "We are going to make a chain that will be used a little later. Cut strips of construction paper and make loops by stapling them together. Let's make as large a chain as we can. However, to make a point, while working, I would like you to wear the gloves you've chosen."

Distribute materials and let the group begin. You may wish to subdivide into several groups with several scissors, staplers, etc. The young people may find the experience fun and possibly more than a little frustrating. After five to ten minutes, stop the activity and have the participants exchange gloves with someone. Tell them that they can get their own gloves if they would like, but it is not required. Continue working for another five or ten minutes. Before finishing, connect all the chains into one big chain. Connect the two ends of the one big chain, making a circle. Set it aside for the closing worship.

Chain Reactions

(Estimated time: 15 minutes)

Encourage group members to talk about their experience. Use these questions to get people started:

1. Did any of you find the experience frustrating? If so, why?
2. Did it make a difference after you exchanged gloves? Why?
3. When you traded, did you get your own gloves? Why or why not?
4. What made the work easy or difficult?
5. Do any of you have a special pair of shoes or an article of clothing that you like especially well? What makes it special?
6. Talk about a funny experience you've had with an article of clothing that didn't fit.

THE GIVING BOOK

Close the discussion by saying something to the effect: "We all are different. We all have different-sized hands, different needs, and different situations throughout life. The times in life which are least frustrating and most rewarding are those when things fit our individual needs. To see what God does about our individual concerns, we are now going to look at two passages of Scripture."

Understanding II | *God recognizes our individuality.*

Give Individuality a Hand

(Estimated time: 30 minutes)

Divide the group into two or more small groups. Assign each group one of the following passages of Scripture:

1. Mark 7:32–38, Jesus heals the deaf man.
2. Luke 19:1–9, the story of Zacchaeus.

Tell the groups that they are to read the passage. Then they are to act out the story for the other groups, using the gloves they brought from home. Allow some time for the group to select their gloves and plan how they will tell the story. The gloves can be used as puppets or with hand motions. You can easily create a stage area by turning a square or rectangular table on its side. Afterward, you may wish to briefly discuss the passages. Use the following questions for help.

1. What did Jesus do that showed he treated people as individuals?
2. Think of other instances and parables when Jesus treated people as individuals (prodigal son, woman at the well, good Samaritan, and others). Talk about them.
3. Is God personal with us? How?

God Knows Us Better Than We Know Ourselves

(Estimated time: 10 minutes)

For this next activity, you will need several old ties, combs, old large man's shirts, food such as cereal or English peas, eating utensils, juice, and cups.

Set the background by saying, "We are the persons who best know ourselves.

Because of this we can do certain things for ourselves more easily than others can do them for us." Have the group list the activities that fall under this category. Some activities might include brushing our teeth, eating, buttoning our buttons, tying ties, putting on makeup, combing hair, and getting a drink, to name a few.

Next let several members of the group pair off and have one person in each pair try to feed, tie a tie, put on a shirt, give a drink, or comb hair for the other person. The person to whom this is being done is to offer no help. After a few minutes, reverse the roles. Then let individuals do the activity for themselves. Talk about the experience.

Close the discussion by pointing out that God knows us even better than we know ourselves. If we are this skilled in taking care of individual needs, one can only imagine the individuality with which God cares for us.

| *Understanding III* | *God's love for us is tailor-made, meeting our needs and fitting our situations.* |

Tailor-Made Gifts
(Estimated time: 10 minutes)

Give the young people pencil and paper. Have them list one or more gifts they have received that seemed perfect or fit them like a glove. Each person is to write down what it was, whether it was a gift of words, a gift of time, a gift of touch, or an object. Then have participants list who gave it to them, and try to put into words why it fit like a glove. Ask them to do the same thing for a gift that they have given. Share the results in small groups.

God, Our Link to Strength
(Estimated time: 15 minutes)

For closing worship, have the group sit in a circle around the chain made earlier. Each person is to hold one link. Talk about how God's love takes us as individuals and gives us strength. Continue pointing out that, while God loves us as individuals, God also brings us together to share the love we have been given. When we link our strengths, we gain from being loved as individuals. We are also enabled to do and bear things that are beyond us individually.

Close with a prayer, thanking God for the tailor-made love given to us. Ask God for help to share the love we have been given.

THE GIVING BOOK

12

The Denial of Gifts

A SENIOR HIGH
PROGRAM ON
DENYING OUR GIFTS
THROUGH COMPARISON

Materials Needed
Four blue ribbons
Newsprint and markers
Pencil for each person
Paper for each person
Paper bag

If we are anything, we are individuals. The fact that God made us each as a startling original serves as a source of some of life's greatest joys. Yet when twisted and distorted, our originality may also bring great pain.

In the fifth grade I discovered love, and her name was Linda Browning. Nowhere had God created anyone more beautiful, or so it seemed to my ten-year-old eyes. One day I tried to tell her this over shared Hostess Twinkies that came from my lunch box. Right in the middle of my telling her, Ronnie Lewis came up to Linda and said, "Let's go to the swing set." She did not say anything. She did not have to. As Ring Lardner would say, "She gave him a look you could pour on a waffle." Then Linda was gone, leaving me with a half-eaten Hostess Twinkie. For a long time I wondered what Ronnie Lewis had that I did not have.

You have wondered the same thing yourself. The world is full of opportunities for these kinds of musings. Why did her project get an A? What makes everyone like him? How did she get the promotion? But these are not the questions to ask. In each of them lies the seed of comparison. Comparison kills. It kills confidence and allows doubt to grow. Comparison extinguishes trust and breeds suspicion. Instead, the questions are, what do I have? Which of the many different gifts has God given me? Let us remember all of us have gifts and are a part of God's plan.

The denial of gifts and the discovery of gifts go hand in hand. This chapter looks at the destructiveness of comparison and the denial of gifts. The next chapter focuses on an authentic discovery of our own gifts.

A Contest of Sorts

(Estimated time: 45 minutes)

Prepare for the first activity by securing four blue ribbons and clearing the furniture from a large room. A carpeted room is desirable though not essential. Divide young people into at least three groups of equal size, plus another group which should have three to five people. The smaller group will serve as the town council. Have groups sit together and introduce the session by saying, "We are going to discover one way that we deny the individual gifts God gives us."

Understanding I | *Comparison is destructive and debilitating.*

Begin the first activity by reading the following: "The town of Pine Bluff has been given an anonymous grant of $100,000 to beautify the city square. For a long time the town council has discussed what to do with the money. Finally they have decided to make the square beautiful by adding certain pieces of sculpture. In order to determine which sculptures will be chosen, the town council plans a contest. The council has set certain standards and invited sculptors from throughout the country to come for the competition.

"You are the sculpture construction teams [indicate the larger groups]. In a moment, the town council will tell you which sculpture to build. When you get your assignment, build the sculpture out of yourselves, using your bodies to make a representation of the objects. The town council will then view the sculptures and award a blue ribbon in each round. The sculpture team gaining the most blue ribbons will win the contract to beautify the city square. Your first assignment is to build a fountain.

"You are to serve as the town council [indicate the one smaller group]. While the sculpture crews are getting organized, we will need to have a council meeting."

Take the council away from the rest of the group. Make certain the other groups cannot hear. Tell the council to use the following standard for judging the sculptures: the group with the most people wearing tennis shoes will win every round. If there are groups with equal numbers of people wearing tennis shoes, select another completely arbitrary standard such as the group with the most blond-haired people. The council keeps secret the criteria for awarding the ribbon until the game is complete. Have the council play their part

enthusiastically. They should carefully scrutinize and inspect each statue when it is complete. After each round, award the blue ribbon and have someone on the council announce, "Don't worry if you didn't win. There are still other opportunities."

Other sculptures might include a rider on a horse, the founder of the city, and a tree. The game is over when the four rounds are completed. For debriefing, redivide the young people into new small groups so that the council members are mixed in with the sculpting teams. First, have the small groups guess what criteria was used in judging the sculptures. Then explain how the winner was actually chosen. Next have the small groups list on newsprint the feelings they experienced while playing the game. After doing this, use these questions for discussion:

1. When did comparisons take place in the game and between whom?
2. Was it a help or a hindrance to be compared? Why?
3. Does the game serve as a mirror of life in any way? Explain.

Move beyond the game, using this set of questions.

1. What are the situations in which we are compared?
2. Who are the people with whom we are compared?
3. Who are the people with whom we compare ourselves?
4. What things do we use to make comparisons?

Let small groups give reports to the others, sharing how they answered the questions. Ask the large group to list and discuss the dangers of comparison. Possible answers might include alienation, defeat ("I can't do it as well as they can"), poor self-image, anger ("it's unfair that I'm compared to them"), jealously ("they're better off than me."), guilt ("why am I successful when they aren't?"), and frustration.

From Comparing to Sharing
(Estimated time: 20 minutes)

Return to small groups of six or seven people, and have someone in each group read 1 Corinthians 12:12–26. Give each person pencil and paper. Explain that one of the best things we can do with a negative action such as comparison is not to deny it but to turn it into something positive. Tell the group that they are going to turn comparing into sharing.

Have each person complete this sentence on paper for each individual in their group. "One part of the body of Christ that ___(person's name)___ is that I would enjoy being is ___(body part)___ because _____
_____." Encourage them to be positive. When the sentences are complete, let people in groups share their responses about one person. After finishing with that person, go to the next person and do the same until everyone has had a turn.

Closing Worship
(Estimated time: 20 minutes)

In preparation, make sure everyone has a pencil and several sheets of paper. The leader will need a paper bag.

CONFESSION

LEADER: "Confession is an act of recognizing who we are and where we are. Part of where we are is that we compare ourselves with others. We also compare one person to another. I want each of you to think about the comparisons you make."

ACTION: "Write down the things you compare. Complete this sentence as many as seven times, 'I am not as _____.'
For example, "I am not as pretty as Kim."

LEADER: "We deny our gifts, thinking others are better than we, but God shows us a better way. We don't need to compare any longer."

ACTION: Have the group tear the comparison sheets into small pieces. Collect the scraps in the paper bag.

LEADER: "Our old ways are gone, taken away like dust in the wind."

ACTION: The leader then scatters a few of the torn pieces of paper by flinging them from his or her hands.

ASSURANCE

LEADER: "God made you as you are for a purpose. The Lord compares you to no one. God only has *only* children. From this moment on, you are free from ever doubting your importance to God. Let us celebrate!"

ACTION: The leader then tosses out the torn paper over everyone, using it like confetti. Or the leader could give handfuls of confetti to the group and they throw the paper in the air.

AFFIRMATION

LEADER: "Each of us has unique gifts. Let us begin the journey of discovering ours."

ACTION: "Write down an affirmation of your gifts by completing this sentence as many as seven times: 'Thank you for making me _____.' For example, 'Thank you for making me patient.'"

LEADER: "God made us what we are. To affirm our gifts, let us thank God using the sentences we have just written. As we pray, the end of each sentence will be different for each of us. This is the way God is with us. We have been given unique gifts; therefore, each of us ends up a little differently."

ACTION: The leader begins, saying, "God, hear our gratitude for our uncomparable gifts. Hear our prayers. 'Thank you, God, for making me _____' [the last sentence is repeated seven times]. Amen."

13

Discovering Our Gifts

Materials Needed

Large pan (or pans) in which to cook soup

Soup stock and seasonings

Knives, potato peelers, stirring spoon(s)

Bowls and spoons for everyone

Pencils for everyone

Copies of *The Gift List* for everyone

Stapler

Small sack for everyone containing perhaps yarn, beads, construction paper, glue, scissors, spools, paper cups, uncooked macaroni, empty egg cartons, apples, markers, pieces of styrofoam, straws, toothpicks, marbles, paper tubes, pieces of felt or material, scraps of wood, pipecleaners, clear plastic wrap, tape.

Sometimes it seems our destiny is to go through life feeling barren. Emptiness and the sense of being giftless are all-too-common experiences. To fill this void, we create our own feeble ways to assure us that we are somebody and have what it takes.

There used to be a time when blue jeans were just blue jeans. The only name on them was yours. Your mother sewed it on the inside so that you wouldn't lose a pair at camp. Lately we have passed through a period when we have been up to our rears with Gloria Vanderbilts and Calvin Kleins, designer names assuring others and us that we have got the right stuff. Even at the grocery store we now have preferred and ordinary canned goods. A can of peas used to be a can of peas. Now along with the familiar Green Giant peas, there is a cheaper, inferior-looking, generic can. You don't have to tell me which kind to buy, and I promise I'll look the other way if our shopping carts should ever meet. The subtle implication is that one kind is better and superior over the other, and that those who buy the preferred stock inherit some of the status.

Why do we concern ourselves with these things? It is because we want to amount to something, to have status. We want to be seen as gifted. In short, we want to be somebody. The words of Paul in 1 Corinthians 12:4–11 pale our weak attempts, and at the same time offer great reassurance. We all have value and a special task: "In each of us, the Spirit is manifested in one particular way, for some useful purpose" (1 Cor. 12:7, NEB). There is no question we have been given unique gifts. Our calling is to discover the gifts that are ours and to use them.

The discovery is more often a process than an event. Sometimes it seems to me we are the strangest part of creation, stranger even than hippos and horned-toads, orchids and otters. Why? Because among all creation, we are the only creatures left unfinished. All the others have well-rounded, predictable outcomes. We, on the other hand, are incomplete. Through the process of discovering, believing in, and using our gifts, we choose what we can become. We can encourage the budding of a new gift or prune back the dreams of our hearts. This chapter seeks to help young people in the exciting process of discovering their gifts.

What then will we become? Let us listen to the stirrings within us. What is inside longing to be born? God has given us our gifts. We need take no other's judgment of worth. We are to discover our gifts and share them with a waiting world.

Getting Started

Group Soup
(Estimated time: 30 minutes)

In preparation for the event, the Senior Highs are to each bring a vegetable or an ingredient for a soup. It is most fun when you do not specify which ingredients to bring but let the young people bring what they would like. You can make suggestions such as spices, a vegetable, or their favorite ingredient but be intentionally vague. The soup you create will be a unique product of each individual's gifts. A variation of the group soup is to have everyone bring an ingredient that is representative of them in some way. Then, over enjoying the hot, steamy bowls of soup, each person can explain what they brought and why.

The soup will be best if it has the longest possible time to simmer and boil, blending the flavors. To aid in this, it will be helpful if you have the soup stock hot and boiling before the young people arrive. Use whatever you like for soup stock, but plain water with a little salt or a few seasonings is sufficient.

As the group arrives, let everyone wash and cut their vegetables, preparing their contribution for the soup. In addition to the hot stock, supply knives, potato peelers, and a stirring spoon. Once the preparation of the soup is complete, have the group move from the kitchen into the regular meeting room.

You will also need to make some advance preparation for the other activities. You will need pencils and copies of the gift list for everyone in the group.

Also have enough small sacks so that each person who comes to the meeting will have one. Fill each sack with one or two of the objects listed in the Materials Needed list. Feel free to include other contents not listed. Fill and staple sacks so that their contents will be a secret until the sacks are opened. Set them aside until needed.

Understanding I | *God has given each of us many gifts.*

Gifts Galore
(Estimated time: 20 minutes)

Once the group is in the room, introduce the session by saying, "Last week we focused on some of the ways we deny our gifts. Today we are going to work on discovering some of our gifts." Introduce the activity by reading 1 Corinthians 12:4–11. Tell the group to divide into small groups and that their task is to make an object representing the passage that was just read. Point out that it will be helpful to get a variety of materials in their small groups. Have a Bible for each small group to refer to while working on their project. Distribute the sacks and let people open them, and divide into smaller groups.

Once the groups are formed, take time for introductions. Have people tell a way in which they are like the object they have in their sacks. The person with the yarn or the scissors begins. For the next step, members within the group trade objects to get one that gives a more accurate representation of themselves if they would like. The group is then to arrive at a consensus of how each person's object reflects his or her unique gifts.

Understanding II | *God calls us to discover our individual gifts.*

Making a Gift List
(Estimated time: 20 minutes)

The group sets the objects aside for the moment. Distribute copies of the gift list that follows this activity. Tell the participants to check the gifts on the list that they feel they have been given. Persons in the group are to select four of the gifts they check to share with others and give an example of their using that gift.

Ask the small groups to build a creative expression of the passage with the objects from their sacks. When these are complete, put the creations in the middle of the larger group so that everyone can see them. Let one from each small group serve as spokesperson to explain the group's work.

Understanding III	*Through using our individual gifts from God, we can create things together that cannot be done alone.*

Souper Supper

(Estimated time: 20 minutes)

Celebrate by serving your group soup. Point out that the soup is a unique creation and that it gets its special flavor from the gifts each person has brought. If one gift were left out, the soup would not taste the same.

Giving Thanks

(Estimated time: 5 minutes)

Close the session with a prayer, thanking God for the good gifts in each of us. In the prayer allow a time where individuals can share the gifts for which they are thankful.

THE GIFT LIST

"In each of us the Spirit is manifest in one particular way, for some useful purpose" (1 Cor. 12:7, NEB).

Check the gifts listed below that you feel you have been given by God.

____Intelligence	____Dreamer	____Athletic
____Humor	____Enjoys hard work	____Cooking
____Musical talent	____Ability to teach	____Practical
____Acting	____Ability to lead	____Realistic
____Sensitivity	____Peacemaking	____Spontaneous
____Compassion	____Artistic ability	____Being a friend
____Integrity	____Loyalty	____Gentleness
____Honesty	____Supportive of friends	____Strength
____Problem solving	____Easily approachable	____Patience
____Enthusiasm	____Willing to take risks	____Kindness
____Listening	____Efficient	____Giving
____Easy-going	____Good with children	____Courageous
____Organized	____Work well with hands	____Cautious
____Mechanical skills	____Pays attention to details	____Affectionate
____Creativity	____Willingness to do thankless jobs	
____Dependability	____Ability to express self in words	

____Any other you might think of

14

Healing in Our Hands

A friend planned a retreat for the staff of a metropolitan ministries program where he serves as director. The retreat's purpose was for people to become better acquainted. Administrators reasoned that if the staff could see each other as fellow human beings and learn to appreciate one another, then they could be more of a team. There would be fewer hassles and increased productivity at work. The staff's one request for the retreat was "We don't want any of that touchy, feely stuff."

Their attitude is understandable. In some circles of the church and other places, we can no longer start a meeting without holding hands, rubbing backs, or something, all in the name of getting to know one another. Sometimes these activities feel more like gimmicks. They smack of false and forced intimacy. No one likes the artificial sweeteners of life—and yet no one can do without the real ones either.

We initially resist the idea of touching one another. While some group-building exercises seem strange, one sometimes wonders if our guard is not up a little too high. Our fear of intimacy keeps us apart. We need to touch, to hold, and to be held. Touch nourishes us and makes us feel good. Yet, in our culture, touch sometimes seems all but forgotten. The loving therapeutic use of our hands is quickly glossed over in this scientific, mechanical, and frequently inhuman age.

Some years ago a study was done. Pairs of males from various cultures were put in a room. They were told to talk and get to know each other as deeply as possible in a half hour. The people conducting the experiment then counted the number of times the two people touched. The Arabians were on the top of the scale. They touched one another more than eighty times. On the other end—you guessed it—the American men touched each other twice and apologized for one of these. We wonder why we have a hard time with touch.

In the fifth chapter of Luke, Jesus healed a leper by touching him. The incident teaches us two things. First, touch is a transfer of energy. Something inside Jesus was shared with the leper. Christ reached out his hand and in that act gave a part of himself to the one in need. When Jesus gave a part of his warmth, the leper's life was better. He was healed. In giving a part of himself away, Christ included the outcast. Touch transfers energy. It is making a connection of what is in me to what is in you. For a moment when we touch, we are brought together and share what we have. What we give just might be what someone needs to have a better life or better day.

Secondly, touch heals us when we are incomplete and torn apart. Christ touched the untouchable. His hand went to the one from whom everyone else would have shrunk. He gave of himself, and the leper had new life. Touching the isolated is our privilege. We have in our hands the most powerful antidote known to loneliness. When we hold one another, we hold with the arms of God. Through our flesh, others can feel the life-giving energy of God's love.

Michelangelo's marvelous painting of creation graces the Sistine Chapel's ceiling. If one part may be singled out, it is where the hand of God in creation reaches toward humanity. There, as the fingers meet, we are given God's touch. This is our calling, to extend our hands and arms, to touch and be touched. This chapter provides the framework for sharing God's gift.

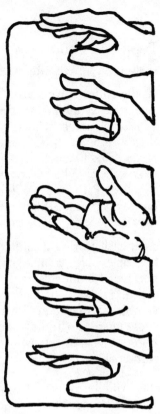

AN ACTIVITY FOR YOUNG PEOPLE DISCOVERING THE VALUE OF TOUCH

Materials Needed
Newsprint
Construction Paper
Tape
Markers
Pencils or Pens
Paper
Bibles

People to People
(Estimated time: 15 minutes)

As the group arrives, play "People to People." Pair off and face each other. Assure the group that it does not matter who their partners are because they will be changing frequently. The leader calls out a position. The partners then assume this position with each other. Positions that can be called include "hand to hand," "elbow to elbow," "wrist to wrist," "nose to nose," "knee to knee," etc. When everyone has assumed one position, then a new position is called. Partners leave the old position and assume the new position as quickly as possible. Start out with less threatening positions such as "hand to hand" or "toe to toe." Gradually go to those which are more risky.

After each pair has been through several positions, the leader calls "people to people." This is the signal to change partners as quickly as possible. Partners then assume the last position they were in before "people to people" was called. The game is most fun when it is played quickly and when you use combination positions, such as "finger to forehead," "elbow to knee," and "nose to ankle." In these, both partners have to assume the position called. For example, in "elbow to knee," both people put an elbow on the other partner's knee.

Talk with the group about playing "People to People." Did some of the positions cause more anxiety than others? If so, which ones? See if the group can express the reasons for feeling the way they do. Record responses on newsprint.

Understanding I | *We are sometimes uncomfortable with touch.*

The Touchometer
(Estimated time: 20 minutes)

Use newsprint or construction paper taped together to create a thermometer-looking device that will stretch the length of the room. Mark the degrees on it.

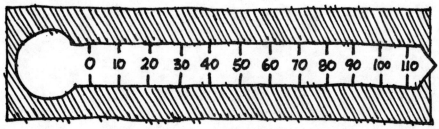

Have the group stand at 72 degrees (the normal comfortable temperature) if there are ten or fewer people. If the group is larger than ten, divide into two or more groups. Let one group watch while the other group responds. Trade places midway in the activity.

Once the group is standing at 72 degrees, pair an activity and a person from the lists below. Ask the young people how they would feel about such an activity with such a person. They respond by standing at certain points along the touchometer. If uncomfortable with the activity, they will move down to the cold (small numbers) end of the meter. If they are very comfortable with the activity, they will move toward the other end of the meter. Discuss their responses. The activity's value is in letting people verbalize why or why not they value certain kinds of touch with certain people.

Touch Activity List	People List
Shaking hands	Someone of the same sex
Squeezing arms	Someone of the opposite sex
Pat on the back	A stranger
Hug	Someone in your family
Kiss	Someone you want to get to know
	A friend
	A girlfriend or boyfriend

A Touchy Subject
(Estimated time: 15 minutes)

On newsprint have the group list the barriers that keep us from using touch to share our care. Discuss them. Barriers might include age, sex, race, physical appearance, cleanliness, lack of familiarity with the person, fear of being too forward, worry over what others might think, a feeling that touch is an expression of only romantic love, family upbringing, or whatever.

Do the same thing again. This time list the openings which give us permission to touch, such as sharing a special moment, approval by culture, and so on. Then have the group rank the barriers and openings from most to least significant. It may be necessary to discuss the rankings in small groups. Ask people to share what they learn.

Understanding II | *A touch is a gift of God.*

Jesus' Touch

(Estimated time: 15 minutes)

You will need Bibles, pencils, and paper for this activity. Have individuals read these passages and answer this question: what does this passage tell us about touch and Jesus? Let people share their responses with the group.

Matt. 8:3	Matt. 9:29	Mark 1:41	Mark 10:13	Luke 22:51
Matt. 8:14–15	Matt. 14:35–36	Mark 3:10	Luke 5:13	John 20:17
Matt. 9:20–21	Matt. 17:6–7	Mark 6:56	Luke 8:43–46	John 20:27

Understanding III | *Touch is healing.*

Keeping in Touch

(Estimated time: 10 minutes)

Encourage the group to reflect for several minutes and try to remember a specific time and person when touch was significant for them. If people cannot think of a time when physical touch was important, they may choose to think of an instance when they were "touched" in some other significant way. Still another option is to think of a person who has touched them many times, e.g., a mother who held someone often as a child. Have the young people write a letter to this person, telling him or her why the time was important to them and what it meant. Share the letters in the group or mail them if you wish.

Touched by God

(Estimated time: 10 minutes)

Close with a brief worship service. Tell the group about the greeting of peace. Explain that the peace greeting, originally the kiss of peace, was a part of the early church (see Rom. 16:16; 1 Peter 5:14). In some traditions it has continued in worship through the centuries. For instance, in the Roman church it is a part of high mass and is seen as a light embrace among the clergy. Others such as the East Syrians are more demonstrative. With this tradition, people hold hands and kiss the person beside them. Methodists, Episcopalians, and others also "pass the peace," especially at communion services.

Encourage one another to share the peace of Christ. Use a hand shake, a hug, or some other form of touch. Say "The peace of the Lord be with you" and respond "And also with you." Thank God for times, places, and people where your lives have been touched. Ask God for the courage to touch one another's lives. A group hug and a benediction are an appropriate ending.

15

The Gift of Anger

A SESSION
LOOKING AT
CONSTRUCTIVE
WAYS TO RESPOND
TO ANGER

Materials Needed

Green, blue, red, and yellow
  balloons, enough for
  everyone to have one.
Five copies of "The Balloon
  Soap Popera"
Pencils
Copies of the *Potential Anger
  Situation* page
Index cards
Bibles (Eph. 4:25–32)
Paper

The trunk lock broke on a young man's car. After 96,000 miles of faithful service, a small spring gave up the ghost. The young man set out to get a replacement. After trips to three places and hearing three identical stories, frustration bubbled up inside him. It seems the spring was not sold separately, which meant that he had to buy a new trunk lock, which meant he needed to buy a new glove compartment lock since the two were sold as one set because they had the same key. One little spring escalated into a $38.75 headache. His blood boiled, and he would not pay. He drove for a week with the trunk lid slapping up and down, but it was better than surrendering. Finally something needed to be done. With a little patience and some needle-nosed pliers, he stretched the spring and fit it back in place. It works to this day.

Life does not always go our way and we are angered. Friends disappoint us, and our needs go unmet. Injustice entraps us, and we are caught with nothing to do but suffer the consequences. A disagreement stirs and words come with the rifle-crack of anger. What do we do? The responses to anger are as varied as the causes. Sometimes anger is returned for anger. Revenge is plotted. We lose our tempers, gain our courage, find our faults, and hide our feelings all in response to anger.

In our culture, anger is often viewed as a non-acceptable emotion. Even the church sometimes perpetrates this myth by labeling anger as sinful. The resulting effect is that anger is dealt with neither cleanly nor constructively. Because we are not supposed to feel anger, we likewise are not allowed to show it. Anger is then turned inward and takes on more subtle forms: depression, overeating, storing it for an uproar, slightly hostile remarks, reckless driving, and others, all of which are destructive.

We need to learn constructive ways to express anger. The Apostle Paul tells us that the denial of anger comes closer to sin than the expression of it. "Be angry but do not sin; do not let the sun go down on your anger" (Eph. 4:26 RSV). If we withhold anger, we sometimes deny ourselves the righteous indignation necessary to change things and to grow into more complete Christians. Being angry is not the issue; what we do with the anger is. This chapter offers an opportunity to learn to accept anger. It provides an avenue to explore creative responses to this emotion with a wealth of power. Whether it is a trunk spring that has been broken or our hearts, creative solutions exist. God calls us to find them.

Getting Started

Situations That Anger Us

(Estimated time: 15 minutes)

Begin by reading the four situations and ask everybody to pick the situation with which they most closely identify.

SITUATION ONE

You and a special friend have planned to go skiing for several weeks now. You have been looking forward to it with great anticipation. Your friend is to pick you up at 9 A.M. The time comes, but your friend does not. Finally at 10:30 A.M. you call your friend's house. Your friend's mother says he has gone skiing and left at 8:30 that morning. In the course of the conversation it becomes obvious that you have been left behind. You thank his mother and hang up. You are extremely angry. You vow that you have a word or two with your friend later, and the words will not be friendly.

SITUATION TWO

Your parents are on your back again at the dinner table about school grades and your personal appearance. They keep attacking you with unfair comments. You feel your heart beating faster, and you want to say something, but you don't. Instead, you sit in silence and after dinner you go to your room and stare out the window. You think about calling your best friend, Ann, but then say, "Why bother. No one cares." You sleep late the next morning and almost miss the bus for school. Once you arrive at school, everything seems boring and you don't have the energy to do anything.

SITUATION THREE

You and your friends decide to play some basketball. About halfway through the game, which you are losing, you begin to notice that your friends seem to be pushing you when you have the ball. They are playing extra aggressively. After a particularly blatant foul, you grab the ball and throw it across the street. You tell your friends to take the ball and their relationships and stuff it, that you never liked cheaters anyway. You then storm home.

SITUATION FOUR

A girl that you thought was a good friend of yours is obviously flirting with a boy whom you have quietly liked for weeks. Later you hear that they have been to the movies and are going again. You are angry and jealous but decide not to let anyone know it. You see the girl in Student Council meeting the next day. The Council is discussing the homecoming dance. She has an idea for the theme. When she offers it, you smile sweetly and say, "That's a great idea. How did *you* ever come up with that?" As you leave the meeting, you think about complimenting her on her hair by saying, "Your hair is such a beautiful color! What color was it originally?" On second thought, you decide not to.

As people make their choices, explain that there are many ways to express anger. Ordinarily, they might respond in a different way than the people in these four situations. But for this and the next activity, encourage young people to pick one of the situations, no matter how foreign it seems. Once the choices have been made, divide the group into smaller groups with one group being those who chose Situation One, another being those who chose Situation Two, and so on. Let the groups discuss their choices. Have them tell one another why they chose the situation that they did.

Understanding I	*There are appropriate and inappropriate responses to anger.*

The Balloon Soap Popera
(Estimated time: 15 minutes)

Give the people who chose Situation One green balloons, Situation Two blue balloons, Situation Three red balloons, and Situation Four yellow balloons. The colors are symbolic. You will also need to select one person from each group to help the reader in involving participants in the activity parable that follows. To do the parable, you will need to have five copies of it—one for each group representative and the reader.

Explain that together you are going to participate in an activity parable. People are to do the *identical* activity with their balloons that the representative from their group does. When the group representatives are seated where everyone can see them, the reader begins.

Story	*Action*
This is the story of Jill, John, Janis, and Jim, four normal people. They grew up in the same town, went to the same church, and attended the same school. They shared the same friends, went to the same movies, even had similar problems. Yet their lives turned out very differently.	
Jill . . .	The green balloon person partially blows up the green balloon and holds the air in. Others with green balloons do likewise.
had typical problems, but she handled them pretty well.	Air is gently released from the green balloons.
Jim . . .	Red balloon person partially blows up the red balloon and holds the air in. Others with red balloons do likewise.
didn't do so well. When things didn't go right,	A little more air is added.
when he got into an argument,	A little more air is added.
when he felt he was treated unfairly,	A little more is added.
he lost control.	The red balloon people release their balloons and let them fly all over the room, and then retrieve them.
Janis . . .	Yellow balloon person partially inflates the yellow balloon and holds the air in. Others with yellow balloons do likewise.
had a different approach. She was a *good girl*. Good girls don't get angry. They are very sweet.	More air is added to the yellow balloon.

So Janis would always smile and say things like, "That's a lovely dress. It would look lovelier, though, on someone who had a little less weight, don't you think?"

John . . .

was the quietest of all four. He didn't say much.

When others would yell at him, he would look sleepy or sad.

Once Jill, John, Janis, and Jim tried out for the school play.

None of them got a part.

Jim got mad, lost his temper, and kicked a hole in the wall of his room, breaking his toe.

Janis said the drama teacher wouldn't have appreciated Shakespeare and didn't know any more about acting than her cocker spaniel.

Jill was disappointed and unhappy, so she found a friend and shared her feelings, even admitting in the process that she was angry. After talking, she felt better.

John only seemed to be depressed.

The people with yellow balloons let the air out of their balloons, but stretch the neck of the balloons from side to side as they do, so the air makes a squealing, squawking noise as it is released.

The blue balloon person partially inflates the blue balloon and holds the air in. Others with blue balloons do likewise.

A tiny bit more air is added.

A tiny bit more air is added again to the blue balloons. The blue balloons stay inflated with people holding the neck of the balloon closed between their fingers.

All balloons are partially inflated except the blue balloons, which already have air.

More air is added to all balloons.

The red balloons are again released and fly everywhere. They then are retrieved.

Air is released from the yellow balloons again, with the squawking noise being made.

Air is slowly and steadily released from the green balloons.

More air is added to the blue balloons.

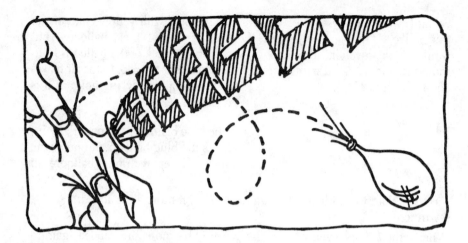

As time passed, the lives of each seemed to take different paths.

Jim started drinking.

He drove too fast

and yelled at his family.

Each time things were getting unbearable he would have a minor tragedy—an auto accident, a traffic ticket, or his wife would move home to her mother.

Someone would have to pick up the pieces.

Janis, on the other hand, seemed to have no one around.

Whenever her malicious tongue was set loose, people would go away.

"That's right, go on without me," she'd say. "It doesn't matter that I'm here all by myself. I'll be okay."

"Don't worry about me. I'll be fine just by myself."

The red balloon is rapidly filled but not to the pint of bursting.

A little more air is added to the red balloon.

A little more air is added to the red balloon, but again not to the point of bursting.

The red balloons are again let go.

The red balloon people retrieve their balloons.

The yellow balloons are partially inflated and the air held in them.

A little air is released from the yellow balloons, causing a squeal, but then it is stopped with some air still inside.

Again, a little air is released, causing a squeal, but then it is stopped with some air still remaining.

The rest of the air is released from the yellow balloons with a squeal.

When John lost his job, he told no one about it. No one asked.	More air is added to the already partially full blue balloon.
When his wife left him saying she thought her husband was hollow inside, John began to believe her and looked sad.	More air is added to the blue balloons.
John once went to the doctor with stomach pains. Ulcers were the diagnosis, but no one could understand. He seemed so slow, so lethargic.	More air is added to the blue balloons.
When someone yelled at John, he didn't yell back. No one understood.	More air is added to the blue balloons.
When John began to stop talking, no one understood. When they found John, no one understood.	More and more air is added to the blue balloons until they all burst.
Jill kept living. She had her problems.	Green balloons are partially filled and held.
But she talked to someone.	Air in green balloons is gently released.
She had maddening times.	Green balloons are partially filled and held.
But she knew without anger there could be no love.	Air from green balloons is gently released.
She had frustrating struggles.	Green balloons are partially filled and held.
But she vented her anger in a creative way.	Air from green balloons is gently released.
And so ends the Soap *Pop*era of Jim . . .	Red balloons are filled and released, enabling them to fly all over the room.
Janis . . .	Yellow balloons are filled and made to squawk as the air is released.
Jill . . .	Green balloons are partially filled and then air is gently released.
and John. Not all of them lived happily ever after.	Silence.

Points of the Parable

(Estimated time: 15 minutes)

Go back into the original small groups and share responses to the parable. Use these statements and questions as a guide:

1. One thing I learned was . . .
2. The balloon personality with which I identified most was . . .
3. I creatively rid myself of anger like the green balloon by . . .
4. A time I felt like the red balloon that flew everywhere was . . .
5. Do you think most people store anger? Explain.
6. Is it acceptable to be angry in our culture? Why or why not?
7. Do you think most Christians see anger as being an acceptable emotion? Why or why not?

Understanding II | *God is not concerned with our anger as much as our responding appropriately to anger.*

Discovering Appropriate Responses to Anger

(Estimated time: 30 minutes)

Distribute pencils and copies of the *Potential Anger Situation* sheet to the group. You will find this at the conclusion of the chapter. Have persons rate themselves concerning the situations. Discuss the results with the group, and see if some of the causes of anger can be identified. The idea is to recognize that we all get angry and that anger is an acceptable emotion.

Create two identical sets of index cards. On each card list an appropriate or inappropriate response to anger. Two cards are to be made for each response. Inappropriate responses include depression, pouting, revenge, suicide, silence, fighting, arguing, hostile comments, overeating, physical violence, accidents, and withdrawal. Think of your own. Appropriate responses include forgiveness, direct communication, negotiation, dealing with anger immediately, sharing anger with an understanding friend, thinking about a solution, and creative actions. Think of your own.

People get one card and try to find their partner who has a card identical to theirs. This is done by communicating nonverbally, acting out the response. Once partners find each other, they discuss these questions:

1. Is the response they have appropriate or inappropriate?
2. Have they ever responded in that way?

Then have partners read Ephesians 4:25–32 and discuss what the passage says about their own anger. Encourage partners to talk about whether or not they find it difficult to get angry and, if so, why. Have them decide if anger is sinful. After the pairs share, they report on their conversations to the group.

Understanding III | *We are called to express anger appropriately.*

Dear Q. Lasa
(Estimated time: 30 minutes)

With pencils and paper, write an anonymous letter to Q. Lasa Cucumber, describing a situation that causes them anger. Start all the letters, "Dear Q. Lasa Cucumber: I am in a pickle." When the letters are complete, put them in a hat or box. Pass the hat or box and have people take a letter other than their own. Then individuals read the letters one at a time. Encourage the group to pretend that they are Q. Lasa and offer their comments on appropriate ways of handling anger.

Close with a prayer for the people facing the situations of anger mentioned in the letter-writing activity.

POTENTIAL ANGER SITUATIONS

Instructions: Circle the appropriate response.
A = Always, O = Occasionally, S = Seldom, and N = Never.

I get angry when . . .

1. I'm around narrow-minded people who think that their way is the only way.	A O S N
2. My parents yell at me in public.	A O S N
3. My friends say they will keep a secret, and they don't.	A O S N
4. Someone tells a racist joke.	A O S N
5. Someone else gets all the credit for something I've done.	A O S N
6. I come in late for a good reason, and my parents don't believe me.	A O S N
7. Someone says, "You shouldn't feel that way."	A O S N
8. My friends get together, and I'm not included.	A O S N
9. I lose.	A O S N
10. The government makes a decision with which I disagree.	A O S N
11. People make fun of me.	A O S N
12. I discover a friend has told me a lie.	A O S N

16

The Gift of Angels— A New Angle

The man paces back and forth. He has trekked from one side of the waiting room to the other so often that a pathway seems worn in the highly-polished floor. Inside, his thoughts fly and skitter in direct contrast to his deliberate steps. "Will she be all right? What will it look like? It? Will it be a boy or a girl? How much longer?" Through bleary eyes, he notices little things; the frayed edges of old magazines, the six leaves on the stem of artificial greenery held secure in the coffee table arrangement's styrofoam base, clock hands that do not move, and the faint touch of his own racing heart. It is this he is trying to hear when the doctor approaches. The words the doctor says are "Mr. Zachman? Congratulations. It's a girl." But what the doctor really means is "Be not afraid. I bring you good tidings."

So goes our stereotypical image of a father awaiting the birth of a baby. Yet, if we are closely attuned to the world, births are not restricted to babies and hospitals. The young boy with sweaty palms reaches for the telephone to call the girl he wants to get to know. The new job is offered and accepted. From within, a quiet resolution comes to stop a destructive behavior so ingrained that it seems like an old friend. The young girl tries to catch her breath before entering the room full of strangers. All of these in their own way are births, and all have common elements. Every beginning, each new start, has fear as its accompanist. We wonder how things will turn out. We do not know if we can do it. We doubt. The temptation in the face of such feelings is to do nothing, just stay where we are. As one wag has said, "You don't fall out of bed when you sleep on the floor."

God's intent for us is growth rather than paralysis, movement rather than stagnation. To help us move and grow in the face of fear, God sends messengers with a word of assurance. Angels frequent times of new birth. The angel came to

Zechariah before John's birth saying, "Don't be afraid" (Luke 1:13). These words echo again from angels speaking to Mary and to the shepherds concerning Jesus' birth (Luke 1:30; 2:10). The angel is there, too, at the empty tomb, telling Mary Magdalene, "You must not be afraid" (Matt. 28:5). An angel comes to Jesus on the Mount of Olives, giving him strength to face the future (Luke 22:43). Elijah meets an angel under the broom tree when he is afraid (1 Kings 19:5–8).

God sends angels to give us the gift of going on. If we will see them, they offer us the courage to say yes to life, but angels are not always easy to envision. We see what we want—and angels don't fit into our current world view. Yet, angels are there nonetheless, holding their glittering wings over us. Someone says to us, "You can do it," or in a conversation we find ourselves suddenly filled with the awe and joy of being alive. With their words, friends help us have the courage we need.

This chapter offers a closer look for discovering the angels in our midst. May your vision be full.

AN EVENING WITH ANGELS

Materials Needed

Tokens for everyone (marbles, poker chips, beans, golf tees, or whatever)

Pencils for everyone

Paper for everyone

Material for a craft activity (poster board, pens, etc.)

Box

Mirror

Copies of "Clarence" for readers

Angel food cake for everyone

Understanding I | *We are afraid of new things.*

Getting Started

The I-Have-Never Game

(Estimated time: 15 minutes)

You will need enough tokens so that each person participating will have five. Use whatever you like for tokens—marbles, beans, or whatever.

As the group arrives, have them sit in a circle. Explain that you are going to play a game called "I Have Never." The object of the game is for individuals to get as many tokens as they can. The game is played in two rounds. In round one people try to complete the sentence "I have never . . ." with something they have not done but that they think that everyone else has done. For example, if one person thinks almost everyone else has water skied, she might say, "I have never water skied." Everyone who *has* water skied gives the girl a chip. Those who have not keep their chips. Let individuals have several turns apiece in each round. If people run out of chips, they can still play, hoping to get their chips on the next turn.

Round two is played exactly like round one except that the sentence is changed to, "Because I'm afraid, I have never . . ."

Clarence: A Messenger of Fear Nots
(Estimated time: 20 minutes)

After the game, explain that today the group will be exploring the things in life (particularly new situations) we fear and how God responds to our fear. To help the group see that God responds to our fears, use the dialogue that follows. It is based on Luke 1:28–31; 2:8–11; Matthew 28:1–7; and Luke 1:46–55. Read these to the group before the dialogue.

Ask readers to read the following parts:

An angel—Clarence	Shepherd 1
Mary—Jesus' mother = Mary	Shepherd 2
Mary Magdalene = Mary M	Shepherd 3
Mary—the mother of James and Joseph, the sons of Zebedee = Mary JJ	

Create three areas. Seat the shepherds in one area; Mary, Jesus' mother, in another area; and Mary Magdalene with Mary the mother of James and Joseph in still a third area. The person reading the angel's part is free to wander among the groups.

CLARENCE: Hello! Welcome everybody. I'm Clarence, A.A. That's for archangel. I understand you want to know something about angels. I thought I'd tell you . . . well, let me just show you. I'll let you see several of my early experiences when I was in training. Now, these happened at different times, but you'll get to see them all at once. One of the benefits of being an angel is that we know no limits of time. So, let's see what happens.

MARY: Who's there? Come in. (*Clarence comes to where Mary is seated.*)

CLARENCE: Mary, good to see you. I've got good news!

MARY: Who are you? You look weird.

CLARENCE: I'm Clarence, an angel.

MARY: That's a weird name.

CLARENCE: Yes, I suppose it is. My mother had this uncle and . . . well, never mind. I've got good news for you! (*Clarence whispers in Mary's ear.*)

MARY: (*Shouting*) I'm what? (*pause*) Pregnant?!

CLARENCE: Now, Mary. Be not afraid . . .

MARY: (Interrupting) What are my friends going to say?

CLARENCE: Well, I suppose they would be happy for you.

MARY: I'm just a teenager.

CLARENCE: With God, age makes little difference.

MARY: (Rolling her eyes) What are my parents going to say? (She is near fainting.)

CLARENCE: Mary—Mary—are you there? Be not afraid. God will take care of you.

MARY: There goes the senior prom.

CLARENCE: Are you listening? I keep telling you, God will take care of those things. Where God guides, God provides.

MARY: Mom didn't want to buy me a dress anyway.

CLARENCE: (Exasperated) Mary! God sent me to you with a special message. But right now the way you're listening, the Lord might as well have sent me to talk to that wall.

MARY: Huh? Oh, I'm sorry. It's just that I'm not used to this idea. I don't know if I'm ready to be a mother. I don't know if I'm ready for God to create new life inside of me.

CLARENCE: Most of us never are.

MARY: (Angrily) Now, how do you know?

CLARENCE: What do you mean?

MARY: Well, you're a boy, aren't you? At least, I think angels are guys. Aren't you? (silence) Boys don't have children. What do you know about new life?

CLARENCE: Mary, it makes no difference.

MARY: Now, what do you mean?

CLARENCE: Well, you see. God creates new life in each of us in different ways. Some of us move to new cities where there is new possibility. We start special friendships. Or maybe it's that we discover our talents for the first time. It's all new life. Some of us even have to get used to new parents like my Uncle Clarence I was named after. You see, his father got sent on a special assignment and . . . (Clarence notices Mary is not listening). What is it, Mary?

MARY: I'm . . . I'm afraid.

CLARENCE: Yes, I see. That's why I came to tell you.

MARY: What's that?

CLARENCE: God doesn't want you to be afraid, and that's why God sent me to tell you to fear not. God wants you to know you're not alone and that God, acting in your life, is something wonderful, not something terrible.

MARY: Sure. All I know is I'm pregnant!

CLARENCE: Mary, just try for a second to . . .

MARY: (*Mary again interrupts.*) If this is so wonderful, show me! (*silence*) Well?

CLARENCE: I'm not sure this is in the rules, but we'll try. I'll show you. You must understand. Angel's standard time is not like human standard time. An angel can come and be gone in a second, (*snaps finger*) and you would never know it except to say, "The day was so beautiful it made me hurt inside." Or, "I can't believe I was able to do it!" On the other hand, an angel can come and stay forever and it's so wonderful it only seems like a second. You see, we're with you when you need us—not at a particular time. So, what I'm about to show you will last only as long as the gleam in your eye. Until it happens, you will know it only in the way you know you had a beautiful dream yesterday morning, but you can't quite recall it. Where you are going, you can see everything, but no one can see you. (*Together they move toward Shepherds 1, 2, and 3, who are sitting in a circle as if huddling around the fire. They are carousing and having a good time until Shepherd 1 spies Clarence. He is suddenly pale, quiet, and frightened.*)

SHEPHERD 1: Oh! Oh, no! (*He rubs his eyes and looks again.*)

SHEPHERD 2: What's the matter?

SHEPHERD 1: I should never have eaten all that goat cheese with the wine. Dear Lord, if you just restore my sight to normal, I'll be good to the wife and kids and I promise never to pig out on goat cheese again.

SHEPHERD 3: What's he going on about?

SHEPHERD 2: I don't know. He needs an Alka Seltzer or something.

SHEPHERD 1: It's just that for a moment over there I thought I saw a person.

SHEPHERD 3: Out here in the dark? Don't be ridiculous!

SHEPHERD 1: You're right. It's just that I've had so many things on my mind lately. No wonder I'm inventing things. My kids have been sick, my wife and I seem to be drifting, and old man Reuben is making noises that he's going to have to cut our pay for watching his sheep.

SHEPHERD 2: (*Angrily*) Reuben! You could have gone all night and not mentioned him. That hook-nosed crook makes my stomach ache.

THE GIVING BOOK

SHEPHERD 3: (*Quietly*) Maybe *you* need the Alka Seltzer.

SHEPHERD 2: (*Angrily*) What's that you say?

SHEPHERD 3: Oh, nothing. Just the mumblings of a shepherd herding sheep in the middle of nowhere, going exactly the same place.

SHEPHERD 1: (*Dejectedly*) You can say that again. Wait a minute! Look! (*Shepherds 2 and 3 look at Clarence for the first time. Suddenly all three are scared and draw back. They cower.*)

CLARENCE: (*Nudging Mary in the ribs with his elbow*) Watch this! (*To shepherds*). "Don't be afraid! I am here with good news for you which will bring great joy to all the people. This very day in David's town your Savior was born—Christ the Lord!"

MARY: (*Joins him, and together they say*) "Glory to God in the highest heaven and peace on earth to those with whom he is pleased." (*Clarence and Mary step back from the shepherds.*)

SHEPHERD 1: Did you see that? I can't believe it! Wow! I've never seen such a sky! Why, the stars are coming alive! Have you—(*Shepherds 2 and 3 are silent, in a daze. Shepherd 1 shakes 2 and 3*) I said, did you see that?

SHEPHERD 2: Wow!

SHEPHERD 1: What do you think it means?

SHEPHERD 2: He said peace.

SHEPHERD 3: (*Incredibly*) He said he was pleased with us.

SHEPHERD 2: Us?

SHEPHERD 1: He said a baby was born to us.

MARY: (*Turning to Clarence*) I thought you said that was my job!

CLARENCE: Shhhhhh! Remember what I said about new life happening to everyone.

SHEPHERD 1: You know, it just came to me. That man or angel . . . anyway, the one with the message, said that the good news will bring great joy to all the people. Do you suppose that means me?

SHEPHERD 1: Do you suppose it means old man Reuben too?

SHEPHERD 3: (*Wondrously*) He said everyone!

SHEPHERD 1: Every time I close my eyes I can still see that, whatever it was. It's like looking at the sun too long. I'm still not sure my eyes are all right. Everywhere I look I see things I didn't see before. (*Looking at Shepherd 2*) Why, your eyes are so gentle, and you (*looking at Shepherd 3*), did you ever notice the beauty of these bushes by firelight? I know something's wrong. I even think I see these smelly sheep in a different way.

SHEPHERD 2: It's the craziest thing. I have this sudden urge to go to Bethlehem and try to find that baby, just to look at it.

SHEPHERD 3: What the hey! It can't hurt. The night certainly won't be any more strange than it's been already.

SHEPHERD 1: Let's go. Say, who was that guy, anyway?

SHEPHERD 2: Why, him? He's an angel! (*The shepherds walk back into the youth group. Mary and Clarence walk toward the other Marys.*)

CLARENCE: What did you think? I always did have a flair for the dramatic.

MARY: I don't know what to think.

CLARENCE: Ponder it in your heart for awhile. Meanwhile, we've got one more moment to see. Come in here. (*Mary and Clarence are beside the other Marys at right angles to them.*)

MARY: What is this? It's dark and damp in here. This place gives me the willies! It's almost like a grave—a grave! Oh, no! You're not taking me off this earth, and I'm not messing with any spirits. Get me out . . .

CLARENCE: (*Interrupting*) Shhhh . . . we're almost there. (*turning to Mary Magdalene and Mary, the mother of James and Joseph*) Good morning, ladies. How can I help you

MARY M: Not at all, unless you want to anoint a dead body.

CLARENCE: Well, actually, I had something else in mind.

MARY JJ: The one who changed us—we want to pay our last respects.

MARY M: Respect. He gave me respect.

MARY JJ: You know, I believed in living again when I was around him. Life was no longer drudgery but a possibility. Believing in him, I never wanted life to end. I believed in him so much I thought that it just might be possible. Well, you see how long that lasted. Now we're back to drudgery, and a final one at that.

MARY M: Wait a minute. Who are you? What are you doing here?

MARY: (*In the distance goes*) Psst . . . (*and motions for Clarence*).

CLARENCE: (*He holds up his hand to stop her. With his hand up, he finds Mary Magdalene and Mary, the mother of James and Joseph looking up into his face. He continues.*) You must not be afraid. I know you are looking for Jesus, who was crucified. He is not here; he has been raised, just as he said. Come here and see the place where he was lying. Go quickly, now, and tell his disciples. (*Mary Magdalene and Mary the mother of James and Joseph put their hands to their faces in astonishment.*)

MARY: (*In the background*) "Pssst!" (*trying to get Clarence's attention.*)

MARY M: My heart cannot take such joy!

MARY JJ: Beauty too rich for words! (*Mary Magdalene and Mary, the mother of James and Joseph, depart. Clarence walks over to Mary, Jesus' mother.*)

MARY: Who were they talking about? (*Clarence is silent, and smiles.*) You mean? Oh, my lord! (*Mary then reads the Magnificat, Luke 1:46–55, RSV. While she is doing so, Clarence slowly leaves, blending into the crowd.*)
"My soul magnifies the Lord,
and my spirit rejoices in God my Savior,
for he has regarded the low estate of his handmaiden.
For behold, henceforth all generations will call me blessed;
for he who is mighty has done great things for me,
and holy is his name.
And his mercy is on those who fear him
from generation to generation.
He has shown strength with his arm,
he has scattered the proud in the imagination of their hearts,
he has put down the mighty from their thrones,
and exalted those of low degree;
he has filled the hungry with good things,
and the rich he has sent empty away.
He has helped his servant Israel,
in remembrance of his mercy,
as he spoke to our fathers,
to Abraham and to his posterity for ever."

Clarence! I understand it all now. I'm not afraid of a new thing! You were right, Clarence. Clarence? (*She turns to find Clarence, and he is gone. She turns to the audience and asks*) Did any of you see a Clarence? At least I think that's his name. No? Surely it was more than a dream. Or was it?

Understanding II | *God sends angels to help us face new things.*

Fearless Fear List

(Estimated time: 15 minutes)

For the next activity, have the young people individually write a list of three to five things that they used to be afraid to do but now can do. Beside each of the former fears they list, have the young people write in who helped them become fearless and how those people helped them become fearless. Next, have them list one thing that they are still afraid to do. Beside this, have people write down what holds them back, who can help, and how they can help. Once this is done, discuss the responses in small groups.

Angel Making

(Estimated time: 20 minutes)

Encourage the group to describe what angels really look like. How are they described in the Bible? Contrast this with the typical representations of angels in art. Next, have everyone make an angel of some type. It may be a drawing or some type of craft activity or perhaps a Christmas ornament.

What Does an Angel Look Like?

(Estimated time: 20 minutes)

Next you will need to have a mirror placed in the bottom of a box. Keep the box where no one can see inside or know that there is a mirror in the bottom. Tell the group that scholars have recently made some new discoveries in researching angels, and that we now have a better idea of what angels really look like. Continue by telling the group that you are going to show them the latest picture of an angel but that you would like them to look at it one at a time and in silence. After taking a peek, they are to silently write their feelings upon seeing the latest picture of an angel.

When the group is quiet, lead each young person to the box. Let each one see his or her reflection. When the whole group has experienced seeing the latest angel and written their thoughts, discuss the experience with them. To stimulate the discussion, have them think of a situation where someone else has been afraid, and they have helped. Ask them also to think of someone who is now afraid and try to imagine how they can help.

Begin the closing worship by saying, "Now we know what angels really look like. Let us keep our eyes open for angels as we go throughout the world. If sometimes you forget to see the angels in your world, use the angels that we have made tonight as a reminder to look again. God sends us angels. Their message to us is "fear not."

Close the worship by singing, "Angels We Have Heard on High," and celebrate by having angel food cake.

17

The Gift of Being Childlike

AN EVENT TO DISCOVER
THE GIFTS OF BEING
CHILDLIKE

Materials Needed

Baby pictures of each person

Favorite childhood snack for each person

Favorite object from the youth's childhood

Childhood Favorite Sheet for each person

Bible for each small group

Song sheets

Old magazines

Poster board

Markers

Copies of "Becoming Like a Child"

The young boy and his father engaged in serious discussion as the car sped down the highway. The magic of taking a trip opened them to each other. First they talked about what the boy liked to do with his time. Then he asked, "Dad, what did you do when you were little?" The father mentioned baseball, an occasional fight, making paper airplanes, playing in the mud, getting into trouble for neglecting to do his chores, snitching cookies from the cupboard, teasing girls, and imaginary space trips taken in a picnic table spaceship. Before he could continue, his son interrupted, "Gee, Dad! You sound like you were a real regular guy. What happened?"

We could ask ourselves the same question. Most of us have left our childhood far behind. In the adult world, not only have we misplaced the activities of children but the traits of that wonderful time as well. Often honesty is now a calculation rather than a natural response. Innocence shows up as a liability in the world of sophistication instead of a goal for which to strive. We seldom live with spontaneity or openness. Childhood days are timeless. Adult days are carefully measured by our wristwatches and counted out accordingly.

It is an unfortunate, if not crucial, loss for those of us who follow Christ. We are told to become like little children in order to enter the kingdom of heaven. Upon hearing this, the first temptation is to try to become more childlike. We say to ourselves, "Let's see. I've got to work more at being spontaneous. I really could do a better job at trusting." And in thinking so, we have once again fallen into an adult world trap. To become childlike is to *be* more than to *do*. It is to respond unguardedly without thinking of the consequences. The activities that follow offer time to be as little children. Use the exercises to discover or rediscover the gifts of your childhood. Even if you only catch a small glimpse, the kingdom of heaven will be closer at hand.

The week before you plan this activity, contact the young people and ask them to bring the following: (1) a baby picture of themselves to you several days before you meet; (2) a favorite childhood snack, enough to share with everyone at the meeting; and (3) a favorite object from their childhood—a photo album, toy, stuffed animal, piece of clothing, or whatever. Only the picture needs to be brought early.

Understanding I | *We lose sight of the value of being childlike.*

Picture This

(Estimated time: 20 minutes)

Before people arrive, display and number the baby pictures you received earlier in the week. You may do this on a bulletin board, table, or in whatever creative way you can imagine. Distribute pencils and paper to individuals as they enter the room. Have them look at the baby picture display and write down their guesses as to who is who.

Childhood Favorites

(Estimated time: 20 minutes)

You will need to have a *Childhood Favorite Sheet* for each person. See the example at the back of this chapter. Divide people into smaller groups. Once they complete the *Childhood Favorite Sheet*, discuss their responses. Let each small group lead the other groups in a childhood game or song.

CHILDHOOD FAVORITE SHEET

As a child, these were my favorites:

Food . . .	Friend . . .
Adult . . .	Story . . .
Place . . .	Toy . . .
Game . . .	Thing to do . . .
Television program or character . . .	Hiding place . . .
Article of clothing . . .	

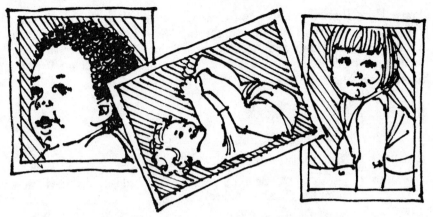

Understanding II | *We are to become like little children.*

The Bible Tells Me So
(Estimated time: 25 minutes)

Give small groups Bibles and ask someone in each group to read Matthew 18:1–6. Use these four statements to explore the passage and guide discussion.

1. To become like a child means . . .
2. A way that I am like a child is . . .
3. A way that I wish I were more childlike is . . .
4. A trait that can be considered childlike is . . .

After finishing, give the groups old magazines, markers, and poster board. Encourage each small group to make a collage representing one of the childlike traits they named in statement four previously. It is important to remember in making the collages that childlike traits are common to all of us, not just children.

Understanding III | *Becoming childlike is found not in trying harder to gain traits of children but in recognizing that God loves us as a parent.*

Becoming Like a Child
(Estimated time: 15 minutes)

Begin a time of worship by singing songs the group learned at church as children. Songs that might be sung include "This Little Light of Mine,"

"Praise Him, Praise Him, All You Little Children," "Jesus Loves the Little Children," "Jesus Wants Me for a Sunbeam," "Jesus Loves Me," "Zacchaeus Was a Wee Little Man," and "We Are the Church." Then pray, giving God thanks for the gifts of childhood. Divide into two groups and close with the following reading.

BECOMING LIKE A CHILD

GROUP 1: Jesus said, "Become like a little child."

GROUP 2: (*Enthusiastically*) That's right! That's good!

GROUP 1: Jesus said, "Unless you become like a little child you will never enter the kingdom of heaven."

GROUP 2: (*Enthusiastically, but then questioning*) That's right! Oh, oh!

GROUP 1: Oh, oh?

GROUP 2: What are we going to do?

GROUP 1: What do you mean?

GROUP 2: We are not little children.

GROUP 1: (*Incredibly*) You're not?

GROUP 2: (*Emphatically*) No way.

GROUP 1: (*Trying to convince*) Sure you are. Being like a child means being innocent. You're innocent, aren't you?

GROUP 2: (*With hesitancy*) Well, not exactly.

GROUP 1: How about open? Children are open. You are open, aren't you?

GROUP 2: (*Sadly*) We wish we were.

GROUP 1: (*Snapping fingers*) Trusting! I know you're trusting.

GROUP 2: We trust everyone. Except our parents. Except our brothers, except our sisters, except our friends, except our teachers, except, except, except, except.

GROUP 1: I see. What about spontaneity? Surely that's true.

GROUP 2: Look before you leap. That's the rule you taught us to keep.

GROUP 1: (*In exasperation*) Surely there must be some way you are like a child.

GROUP 2: Not in the ways that matter, but we'll try harder.

GROUP 1: Harder?

GROUP 2: (*With confidence*) Sure! We'll work at þeing more innocent.

GROUP 1: (*Like you're checking off a list*) Check.

GROUP 2: Put on new spontaneity.

GROUP 1: Check.

GROUP 2: We will make the effort to be more trusting.

GROUP 1: Check.

GROUP 2: We will struggle to be more open.

GROUP 1: Check. Wait a minute. Work? Try? Struggle?

GROUP 2: (*Emphatically and then like a chant*) Check! Work. Try. Work. Try. Work. Try. Work. Try. Work. Work. Work. Work. Work.

GROUP 1: That doesn't sound much like a child to me.

GROUP 2: (*Desperate*) What can we do? It's impossible!

GROUP 1: (*With sudden understanding*) Wait a minute! I've got an idea!

GROUP 2: (*Skeptical*) Yeah?

GROUP 1: Yeah! I know a way that you and even I are like little children.

GROUP 2: (*Still skeptical*) What's that?

GROUP 1: Well, who is your parent?

GROUP 2: Mom and Dad. Who do you think?

GROUP 1: No, I mean, who is your eternal, loving parent?

GROUP 2: Oh. That's easy. That's God. Always—

GROUP 1: Right! And if God is always your parent . . .

GROUP 2: (*Suddenly catching on*) That means we're always God's children!

GROUP 1: Always!

GROUP 2: (*Incredibly*) What do you know? (*Loud applause*)

GROUP 1: Always!

GROUP 2: We don't have to try?

GROUP 1: Do children try?

GROUP 2: What do you know! (*Applause*)

GROUP 1: God, our parent, loves us. We are God's children.

GROUP 2: That's enough. We are God's children. (*Applause*)

Close the evening with individuals sharing their childhood snacks and telling about their favorite childhood objects.

18

The Gift of Time

A man and a woman sit in their easy chairs reading the newspaper. The wife looks at her husband and inquires, "What's today?" He says, "The 5th. Why?" She says, "Sixteen years ago today we built the new set of steps for the front porch." The husband answers, "Your life has been one big thrill after another, hasn't it?"

There are moments that seem like days, days that feel like months, and weeks that last a year. All of us have experienced the instances when time chooses to stand still, the clock's hands refuse to move. Whether waiting in a dentist's office, or for a phone call, we are at loose ends until that for which we wait comes. In other instances, we lose our motivation altogether and become bored. We search for something to do.

By the same token, most of us have a familiarity with the opposite extreme. Some days we feel like Lucille Ball. It seems like every place Lucy ever worked had an assembly line or a conveyor belt. In the particular episode I recall, she removed pies from a belt as they came out of the oven. There was one small problem: Lucy and the belt operated at different speeds. The pies stacked up. Several narrowly escaped falling on the floor. Lucy started balancing two or three at a time. She got her fingers stuck in the meringue. The belt moved faster and faster, and the inevitable occurred. In her haste, Lucy tripped and fell face first in one of the pies. The relentless belt continued. Pies exploded everywhere on the floor. Finally Lucy picked herself up, mess and all, and started again. This time as she loaded pies, she would calmly package one and throw the next away, package another and throw the next away. Lucy was forced to admit her limitations. Like Lucy, there are times when we have our fingers in too many pies. There is simply not enough of time or us to spread around.

Very few people master the appropriate use of time. On one hand we waste our hours filling them with trivia, or even worse, nothing at all. A world awaits, crying for our attention. On the other hand, we pack our lives so tightly that nothing seems to offer any enjoyment. God gives us time. It holds for us the essence of life itself. To do nothing with it is to deny the Giver who calls us to a challenging and abundant life. Each moment offers an invitation if we will only say yes. Yet, to say yes to too many invitations is likewise a denial of the Giver. Bob Raines complained about a crammed schedule to his father, Bishop Richard C. Raines, who "nailed me to the wall with his succinct reply." Said the father to the son, "It is good that you are learning that being a five-foot blade and trying to cut a six-foot swath isn't heroism, but egoism and a subtle form of atheism."

How do we celebrate, share, and enjoy this gift which God has entrusted to us? How can we make wise use of time between the extremes of ignoring God and trying to be God? This chapter does not have all the answers, but it offers a place to start. By becoming more aware of the way we use God's gift of time, perhaps we have taken a step toward our chief end: to glorify and enjoy God forever.

AN EVENING OF
ACTIVITIES EXPLORING
THE GIFT OF TIME

Materials Needed
Oranges (several for each person)
Egg timers
Calendars
Hour glasses
Airline schedules
Watches
Family albums
Anything to do with time
Paper plates for each person
Pencils (preferably orange) for each person
Copy of the *Time Inventory Sheet* for each person

Getting Started

To prepare for the activities, you will need to have a number of oranges. Each young person will use at least one but, if possible, it is better to have several oranges for everyone. Create the proper mood for the event by gathering anything you can think of that has something to do with time. Use your imagination. Bring egg timers, watches, hour glasses, airline schedules, calendars, family photo albums that show people growing up and growing old, and other items. Arrange these around the room for people to see.

Orange You Glad You Asked

(Estimated time: 20 minutes)

As participants arrive, divide them into small groups of five to seven people. Have each group sit in a circle. Explain that the purpose of the evening's activities is to help people take a closer look at what they do with the gift of time. Toss an orange to each small group. Whoever catches the orange will begin the discussion by completing the first statement. When the first person finishes answering the question, she then tosses the orange to a second person in the group. The leader then reads another statement to be completed by the person now holding the orange. He then tosses the orange to a third person. The process continues until all the statements have been completed by someone in the small group. The leader may choose to use the statements a second time in order to get different responses, or to allow all to participate. Below is a suggested list of statements to use.

Time flies for me when . . .

I waste time when . . .

I like to spend time when . . .

Time never ends when . . .

Free time for me is . . .

I could spend a lifetime . . .

There is never enough time to . . .

Something I would do any time is . . .

I have too much time when . . .

I don't have time to . . .

Understanding I | *Time can be abused.*

Orange Overload

(Estimated time: 15 minutes)

Begin the next activity by giving each person an orange. If the group is small, give several oranges to each person. Ask and see if there is an individual in the group whose favorite flavor of fruit happens to be orange. Ask this person to stand. Have group members give this person their oranges, one at a time. Enough oranges should be used to that it will be very difficult, if not impossible, for the individual to hold all the oranges. (Containers are not allowed.)

114   THE GIVING BOOK

If an orange is dropped during the process, have the individual holding all the oranges try to pick up the dropped orange. When the loading is complete, ask the individual to try to sit down and stand up three times in quick succession. Some oranges may spill onto the floor, but this is all right. At any rate, it should be difficult for the individual to hold all of the oranges. Next, have everyone take an orange back from the individual. Thank the person who volunteered to hold the oranges.

Ask the group if the experience in which they have just participated parallels their own use of time in any way. If so, then how?

Encourage the group to share the feelings they experience when they are too busy, e.g., frustration, anger, guilt, doing many things poorly and nothing well, anxiety, pressure, etc. Write the responses on newsprint or a chalkboard.

Orange Concentrate
(Estimated time: 10 minutes)

Next have people place their oranges on a table, chair, or the floor. Explain that their task is to look at the orange and to concentrate on it for five minutes. They are not to speak to each other or to touch their oranges.

Once this has been completed, ask the group if this experience in any way reflects their use of time and, if so, how?

Again, encourage the group to share the feelings they experience when they are bored. Record the responses on newsprint or a chalkboard.

Understanding II | *Time is God's gift.*

A Timely Gift
(Estimated time: 10 minutes)

Once again divide the young people into small groups. Have someone in each group read Ecclesiastes 3:1–11. Use the following questions for discussion.

1. Do you have enough time to do everything you want to do? Why or why not?
2. Do you feel God has given us enough time? Explain.
3. What do you think is meant by the phrase, "He has made everything beautiful in its time" (Eccles. 3:11, RSV).

A Slice of Life—Graphic Discoveries
(Estimated time: 10 minutes)

For the next activity, you will need paper plates and markers (preferably orange) for everyone in the group to have their own. Spruce the plates up a little, giving them the appearance of an orange, by adding a few green construction paper leaves and an orange border. Have each young person make a pie graph with their plates, indicating how they spend their time. The categories would include

A. Sleeping

B. Work or school

C. Time spent having fun

D. Time spent preparing for things— bathing, getting dressed, etc.

E. Time spent in devotion to God

Have the young people share their graphs with the small group. They tell what they would spend more or less time on if they could.

Time Inventory
(Estimated time: 10 minutes)

Duplicate enough copies of the *Time Inventory Sheet* included in this chapter so that each individual has one. When the sheets have been completed, encourage people to discuss them in the small groups. It is interesting to watch the "yes/no" lists. If people have few things listed on their "no" list, then everything they add will mean less time for what they are now doing. If people say no to several things and do not add any yeses, it will mean more free time, which may be what is wanted and needed, perhaps not.

Understanding III | *God's gift of time can be creatively used.*

Creativity with Oranges
(Estimated time: 20 minutes)

For the next activity, have people do something creative with their orange or put it to good use in some way. Let people choose from several alternatives as to what they would like to do or have them come up with their own ideas. You will need to have whatever supplies are necessary for the various activities. Possible things to do with the oranges include eating it, making orange juice, juggling, using the oranges to create a sculpture, giving the orange to a friend, making jelly, creating sachet balls with cloves and other spices, or whatever. Again, use your imagination.

Worship

(Estimated time: 10 minutes)

Close with a brief worship service. Sing "Turn, Turn, Turn." Ask people to make a commitment to better use their time. These commitments might be specific things written down or shared with the group. Pray, asking for God's help to bring these commitments into action. Thank God for the good times and have a period of silence, asking God for strength and help to face the difficult times. Close by singing, "O God, Our Help in Ages Past" or "Circles" by Harry Chapin.

TIME INVENTORY SHEET

Put an "x" on the lines to represent how you spend your time. For example, if you spend most of your time with others, your "x" will go very close to the "others" end of the line. If the time you spend is equally divided between others and yourself, your "x" will go in the middle.

Once you have put an "x" on every line, go back and put an "o" on every line to indicate how you *would like* to spend your time. It may be exactly like you now spend your time or very different.

others————————————————————self

fun————————————————————work

being useful————————————————————being useless

dreaming————————————————————doing

listening————————————————————hearing

List below activities that you want to say yes to and take more time with in your life. When you have finished, list the activities that you want to say no to more often and on which you want to spend less time. List as many as you like.

Yes	No
1.	1.
2.	2.
3.	3.

The Gift of Time

19

Forever Full

AN ACTIVITY DISCOVERING
"WE ARE FOREVER FULL!"

Materials Needed

Empty container for each
person

Plain paper bag for each
person

Magic markers for each
person

Blindfolds for five or six
people

Paper for everyone (enough
sheets to equal the
number of questions)

Pencils for everyone

Beans (ten per person)

Copies of the litany

A father who had been away from home brought his daughter a present. Since the present was small, he had it wrapped in a tiny box. He greeted her with a hug and slipped the present into her sweater pocket without her knowing. "What did you bring me, Dad?" she asked. He responded, "I've brought you a present, but you will have to find it." Immediately she started her search. She thoroughly checked his luggage and looked throughout the house. Finding no present, she became discouraged and returned to her dad. "Where is it, Dad? I can't find it." He smiled and told her to look in the pocket of her sweater. Slipping her hand inside, she discovered the delicately-wrapped box. She had the gift with her all the time, only she did not know.

There is some of that girl in us all. We feel empty and search to find the gifts that make life complete. If we are lucky, somewhere along the way it dawns on us that we have had the gifts all the time. God blesses us with enough even if we cannot see. Our growth is learning that we are continually full. Long ago the tomb was left empty so that we might be forever full. As followers of the way, fullness is our perpetual gift.

This chapter's focus is on discovering that we are forever full. Perhaps with it, you will see your gifts to celebrate and share in a new light.

Getting Started

Name Tag Bags
(Estimated time: 25 minutes)

Have each participant bring an empty container from home. This will be used later to sculpt an altar.

Give people a plain paper bag when they arrive. With magic markers, decorate the bags with (1) your name, (2) times I felt empty, and (3) times I felt full.

After the name tag bags are complete, gather in a circle. Have people share an empty time and a full time. Give an overview of the evening's purpose, using some of the material in the introduction. Pray for God's blessings on your time together. A fitting prayer could be from Paul's letter to the Colossians:

"We ask God to fill you with the knowledge of his will, with all the wisdom and understanding that his Spirit gives. Then you will be able to live as the Lord wants and always do what pleases him. Your lives will produce all kinds of good deeds, and you will grow in your knowledge of God. May you be made strong with all the strength which comes from his glorious power, so that you may be able to endure everything with patience. And with joy give thanks to the Father, who has made you fit to have your share of what God has reserved for his people in the kingdom of light" (Col. 1:9–12).

Understanding I	*We often have a faulty perception of being empty. We are not as empty as it sometimes seems.*

Full or Empty?
(Estimated time: 15 minutes)

Here are two ways to gain understanding of the way we perceive ourselves:

1. Blindfold five or six people from your group. Then bring a large object into the room. A possible object could be an Early American spoke-back rocking chair or some other type of furniture. Lead the blindfolded people to the object. Guide their hands so they touch only a small portion of the object, such as one of the spokes, one of the rockers, or the cushion on the chair. Take the object from the room. Remove the blindfolds and ask the young people to guess what they touched. After guesses have been made, bring the object back into the room. Ask the group, "what did you learn

about the way we perceive things? What does this say about how we see ourselves and others?" See if the group can think of examples in their own lives where they have had a faulty perception of themselves or someone else because their experience was limited. Conclude the discussion with a responsive reading of the poem, "The Blind Men and the Elephant" by John Godfrey Saxe.

or

2. Play the "Match Your Perception" game. Form two teams. Players need pencils and paper to use in answering the questions. This game illustrates that we can all see the same thing but misunderstand what is actually true. Choose an emcee to read the questions to the entire group. Players have thirty seconds to answer. The object is to match the other team members' answers/assumptions.

Here are some sample questions. Make your own to add to the list.

    A. After the basketball game, Teary Terry was crying because . . .

    B. The stay-at-home Stanfords never go on vacation because . . .

    C. Clancey, the classmate, never says hello in the hall because . . .

    D. Munch-out-Minnie never eats chocolate because . . .

    E. The neighbors next door never stop by for a visit because . . .

    F. The children get everything they ask from their parents because . . .

    G. Report-card Rudy gets outstanding grades because . . .

After playing compare perceptions among team members. Ask, "What did you learn about each other? About yourself? What does this say about perceptions?"

Understanding II | *God intends us to know that we are forever full.*

Full Findings
(Estimated time: 20 minutes)

1. Explore Scripture by doing a concordance word study of "full."

or

2. Break into smaller groups, giving each group a reading to study and to share their learning with the rest of the groups. Passages to discover include Colossians 2:6–10, 1 Kings 17:8–16, Psalm 16:5–11, Romans 15:13–14, and John 1:14.

3. Even when we doubt our own abilities, God continues to use us. Use the following story to reflect on fullness and emptiness. Henry Pope Mobley tells an interesting story about his first hospital call. He was substituting for a sick minister, and the church secretary called to tell him that one of the congregation's members was ill and had been in a coma for five days. She said that he should make a visit to the hospital. That was simple enough, but the prospect of going to the hospital terrified him. When he got to the door of the man's room, he was even more frightened. He said,

> The door opened to my knock and I was confronted by thirteen people gathered in an area not much larger than the black hole of Calcutta; the smoke resembled the early morning fog in San Francisco, and the dim faces in the cloud all turned their puzzled eyes on this intruder to their death watch.
>
> I identified myself as from the church and one of the granddaughters kindly took charge and led me through the throng to the bedside where the elderly man lay.
>
> Panic set in. I had no notion about what to do or what to say. Finally, the granddaughter rescued the moment by asking me to say a prayer. I had no idea what to pray, opened my mouth and began reciting the 23rd Psalm. What inspired that is also a mystery; I might have started on, "Now I lay me down to sleep . . .", or "God is great, God is good, and we thank him for our food." But with the opening lines, "The Lord is my shepherd . . .," a kind of heavenly peace settled over that dismal scene. My eyes were closed until another voice picked up those lovely words, "Though I walk through the valley of the shadow of death, I will fear no evil, for Thou art with me . . .". And the old man, who had been in a coma for five days, finished that psalm with me.
>
> After that a kind of loving confusion took over. The patient opened his eyes and began to recognize the faces of his children and grandchildren. I slipped out unnoticed. The Spirit of the living God had been in that room, and I have never been afraid again when visiting in a hospital.[4]

Complete the following statements no matter which activity is used.

    A. One thing I discovered about fullness was . . .

    B. A question I have about fullness is . . .

    C. One thing this tells me about me is . . .

    D. One thing this tells me about God is . . .

    E. One thing this tells me about people feeling empty or full is . . .

| *Understanding III* | *One of the privileges we have is that God uses us to fill the lives of others.* |

Giving Carefully

(Estimated time: 15 minutes)

Use the following game to discover the importance of giving carefully. The group sits in a circle. People use their name tag bags, each filled with ten beans. There will be two rounds. In round one, sing a fast, familiar favorite song ("Oh, When the Saints" or whatever). In rhythm, people remove one bean from their sack and place it in the sack of the person on their right. People start by taking a bean from their own sacks. Pick up the tempo of the song, gradually getting faster and faster. This round may get crazy!

Round two. This time, sing a slow, gentle melody ("Pass It On" or whatever). As gently as possible, pass the beans from one sack to the next, one at a time. After singing one verse, stop.

Talk about the game. Ask these questions.

    A. Did you end up with ten beans at the end of the game?

    B. Which round did you like the best? Why?

    C. What does this say about giving?

    D. What takes away fullness?

    E. What brings about fullness?

    F. How can we be gentle and caring in our giving?

    G. What ways are we careless in our relationships?

| *Understanding IV* | *We can best awaken fullness in others when we know we are full of things to give.* |

A Worship-full Celebration

(Estimated time: 15 minutes)

Use a worship celebration to affirm each person's fullness in Christ. Begin by building an altar from the empty containers. Talk about how, while we may feel empty, we are forever full through the love of Christ. Have young people find a partner. Designate one partner as Group One and the other as Group Two. The group then reads the following litany with partners facing each other.

GROUP 1: O God, at times we see ourselves as empty.

GROUP 2: Forgive our outlooks that are waste-**full**.

GROUP 1: Everliving One, in moments we lose the beauty of your gifts.

GROUP 2: Forgive our seeing life as unevent-**full**.

GROUP 1: Creator, in our days we replace anticipation with dread.

GROUP 2: Forgive our facing your creation in a way that is dread-**full**.

GROUP 1: Maker, in our activitiy, we substitute our ways for yours.

GROUP 2: Forgive our accepting that which is harm-**full**.

GROUP 1: Lord, in all we do and say and see.

GROUP 2: Forgive our being sin-**full**.

(A *time of silence*)

LEADER: There is hope. God knows us as we are and still fills us!

GROUP 1: Mighty One, you jolt us with joy

GROUP 2: That we may be cheer-**full**.

GROUP 1: You touch us with gratitude

GROUP 2: That we may be thank-**full**.

GROUP 1: You encourage us with grace

GROUP 2: That we may be hope-**full**.

GROUP 1: You restore us with a sense of awe

GROUP 2: That we may be wonder-**full**.

GROUP 1: You move us with compassion

GROUP 2: That we may be thought-**full**.

GROUP 1: You fill us with confidence

GROUP 2: That we may be delight-**full**.

GROUP 1: You support us with care

GROUP 2: That we may be peace-**full**.

GROUP 1: O God, you love us without stopping

GROUP 2: That we may be forever full.

ALL: Amen.

Close by singing songs filled with joy and thanksgiving. One possibility might be "Share a Little Bit of Your Love" by Ray Repp.

20

New Life for Seedy Characters

Some years back I helped my little brother learn his multiplication tables. One night we struggled through the two's. We battled as he learned the three's and four's. The five's represented the epitome of drudgery. But when we got to the sixes, something happened. A sudden flash lit his eyes. You could all but see the light bulb come on over his head. In all innocence, he looked up and said, "Hey . . . there's a pattern to all of this, isn't there!"

With the rote ways we travel through life, we are easily dulled to the intricate relatedness of things. A spider weaves a web. One part cannot be touched without sending tremors throughout the rest of it. You are related to me, I to you. One thing affects another. The same is true of death and new life. They are inexorably bound as partners throughout the dance of vitality. One does not happen without the other. We easily see the beauty of a birth, a new start. We celebrate new life as it breaks forth among us. We rejoice with each conquered old habit. An alcoholic struggles mightily and stays sober. A friendship forms, easing the pain of love lost. New scientific advances make old ways obsolete.

Much harder to see is the dying that must take place for new life to be. With each new growth a piece of the old must be given up. In order to embrace new life, we must first let go of the old ways we hug. The pattern continues throughout; beginnings are intertwined with endings, dying accompanies being born. The binding of new life with death stands at the center of our faith.

Death was the first ending of the story. Christ died. The dreams and hopes of his followers lay scattered on the ground. They held as much life as the palm branches cut for a parade now withering in the sun. Who could have seen the cruel twist of fate that would end the week? Now Mary went to the tomb. She waited until the Sabbath ended, for travel was not permitted on the Sabbath. The night grew long, too long. She rose sometime between 3:00 and 6:00 that morning. Walking through the graying of the morning, she must have thought about the unreconciled hope. Yesterday he was; today he was no longer. Still she clung to something. She returned to where he was, being faithful at a time when faith made no sense. Here the story takes an unexpected turn. The stone was rolled away from the tomb! She summoned Peter and John; together they went to the empty grave. The meaning was dissolving into mystery. Death was fading into new life. The ending was no ending.

There is a pattern to all of this, for them and for us. The resurrection of Jesus Christ is God's ultimate triumph of life. Just when life absolutely makes no sense, something breaks anew. Parts of life must die, but death always gives way to life. God's love promises another twist of the path, and love and joy will bloom where ashes have been.

This chapter looks at the seed, a metaphor Christ used to look at his own death and new life. Follow the image and make your own discoveries. May you be eased through your dyings and led to new life in Christ.

AN ACTIVITY ENABLING YOUNG PEOPLE TO EXPERIENCE THE JOY OF NEW LIFE AND RESURRECTION

Materials Needed

Newsprint

Markers

Sleeping bags

Pencils

Paper

Phonograph and record or tape and/or tape player

Flower pot for each person—can be styrofoam cups

Things with which to decorate pots

Large variety of seeds

Potting soil

"Seedy" snacks—popcorn, sesame bars, nuts, or whatever

Getting Started

Come Up with as Many Ends as You Can
(Estimated time: 10 minutes)

Divide the young people into two teams. Each team forms a line by people putting their hands on the hips of the person in front of them. Explain that the object of the game is to try to get the other team's end (the last person in line), while protecting your own end. An end is captured when the first person in line touches the other team's end with both hands while spelling "e-n-d." Only the first person in line may capture the other team's end. The captured end becomes the first person in line for the team that captured the person. Both teams try to get the other team's end at the same time, and just about anything goes as long as no one lets go of the person in front of them. Add people as they come, and play until everyone has arrived.

An Endless List of Ends
(Estimated time: 10 minutes)

Divide the young people into two teams, and give each team newsprint and a marker for writing. Introduce the evening's theme by saying, "We are going to take time to explore the possibility of new life. Fresh starts and new beginnings are one of the best gifts we can ever receive. However, in order to receive new life we sometimes must first let go of the things we hold on to. Birth is seen as a natural part of life. While we do not often think so, dying and endings are, too. The next activity will help us look at some of the endings in life."

In a period of four minutes, the two teams are to try to list as many endings in life as they can. Examples could include graduation, a store going out of business, divorce, the benediction at the conclusion of the worship service, breaking up, the death of a loved one, taking down the Christmas tree, and others you may imagine. After the time ends, the groups share their lists with each other.

Understanding II | *Sometimes parts of us must die that we might live again.*

An Experience: From Dying to Living
(Estimated time: 15 minutes)

For the activity that follows, each young person will need a sleeping bag, pencil, and paper. Spread the sleeping bags on the floor. You will also want to have either a phonograph and record or a tape and tape player. Explain to the group that what is to be done next offers a way for them to let go of

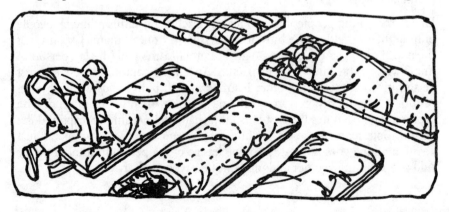

something that bothers them or keeps them from living the new life intended for them by God. Ask the young people to individually and silently write one or two things of which they wish to let go. Maybe it is a bad habit, a hostile feeling, or a nagging problem. They will not have to share these with anyone. Next, have young people fold their responses and firmly hold the folded paper in one hand. Have the young people gradually and deliberately get into their sleeping bags to appropriate background music. Encourage them to take their time. When people are inside, have a brief period of silence. Then read the following dialogue with another person.

PERSON 1: "Listen to these words of Christ: 'A grain of wheat remains a solitary grain unless it falls unto the ground and dies; but if it dies, it bears a rich harvest'" [John 12:24, NEB].

Silence

PERSON 2: "You are the seed fallen to earth. Let go of that part of you that keeps you from growing, from going on to new life."

Silence

PERSON 1: "Now I would like you to let go of the paper you hold in your hand. Place it beside you in the sleeping bag."

Silence

PERSON 2: "You are the seed. The light calls you to grow."

Silence

PERSON 1: "Anyone who is in Jesus Christ is a new person altogether. The past is finished and gone. Everything is fresh and new."

Silence

PERSON 2: "You are the seed. Come from the earth."

Silence

PERSON 1: "For in Adam all die, so also in Christ shall all be made alive" [1 Cor. 15:22, RSV].

Silence

PERSON 2: "You are the seed. Come to new life. Bear a rich harvest."

PERSON 1: *Use the record player or tape recorder again and play instrumental music that is inspiring and hopeful. The themes from "Chariots of Fire" or "Jonathan Livingston Seagull" would be good selections.*

PERSON 1: "Now it is time for us to come from the earth. I would like you to slowly, gradually, creatively come out of your sleeping bags. Imagine you are a seed, coming to life. Let your movement reflect the growth. Picture yourself as if you are free of a burden for the first time in many months. Let your coming out show your new-found freedom."

Parable Pots

(Estimated time: 20 minutes)

Have flower pots and decorative material ready for the next activity. Almost anything could be used for flower pots: coffee cans, jars, styrofoam cups, or clay pots themselves. Decorate pots with paints, wrapping paper, magic markers, or whatever. When the creative movement has ended, let each person decorate a pot. Use the decoration to illustrate the new parts of life people want to claim.

Understanding III | *Christ rose from the dead so that we might have a new life.*

Planting Seeds of Celebration

(Estimated time: 20 minutes)

Divide people into small groups. Give each small group a Bible and ask someone to read Romans 6:1–11. Pay special attention to verse 4. Have participants remember one new thing (although it may no longer be new) that being a follower of Christ has brought into their lives.

Gather a large variety of seeds and potting soil. Use seeds of different colors and textures. Each seed should be one that will sprout with minimum care, such as beans or marigold seeds. Let people pick a seed that represents the part of themselves that they would like to see coming to new life. Ask people to share why they selected their particular seed and what it represents to them. Afterwards, plant the seeds in the pots.

Worship

(Estimated time: 5 minutes)

Close the program activity with worship. Sing "The Rose" from the movie of the same title because of its reference to seeds in the first verse. Pray, asking God for help and guidance with new life.

Seedy Snacks

(Estimated time: 10 minutes)

After worship, serve snacks. It is fun to use a wide variety of seeds in your treats, such as sesame bars, popcorn, sunflower seeds, pecans, or corn nuts.

21

The Gift of Darkness

A YOUTH NIGHT
DISCOVERING
THE GIFT OF
DARKNESS

Materials Needed
Blindfold for each person
Paper for each person
Pencils for each person
Two blank 3″ × 5″ cards for
    each person
Candles
A small lamp

None of us is ever totally strong or helplessly weak, and none of us ever has life "all together." God has placed in each of us a delightful combination of strengths and weaknesses that support us and move us toward growth and meaning. We are made a little lower than the angels, yet each of us has a thorn in the flesh. Our strengths affirm us and let us know we have value. While we are not always aware of it, the same possibilities exist in our weaknesses. The gift of our weaknesses grants us the possibility of becoming. Through our struggles, we learn that we are ever unfinished and have the challenge to be the best human beings we can be.

A star-filled night can be an overwhelming experience. The shafts of light move through the eyes to sear our souls. But what we forget while being held in awe of the stars is that the surrounding blackness has beauty as well. It holds a mystery of unmeasurable depth. It enfolds us, inviting us to come in and discover the subtleness, the sameness. We are called to move through the darkness and learn. And if we have the courage to face the unknown, we shall find ourselves on the other side of night and find meaning on the other side of mystery.

This youth experience is an adventure to move from our darkness into light and to see the gift of our weaknesses. The invitation is yours, and along the way, who knows, you might just discover a fellow traveler.

Being in the Dark

(Estimated time: 20 minutes)

Have the youth gather at their regular meeting place. As they come in, blindfold each person. When everyone has arrived, begin by saying, "All of us have been in the dark occasionally. From time to time we each have had a struggle or a weakness to endure. Tonight we are going to look at some of the dark places in us."

Next have the group join hands and lead them single-file into a darkened room. This might be the room where the choir robes are stored, the basement, or whatever. Prepare it in advance by removing anything that could hurt someone if they bumped up against it in the dark. You will want to take out anything that could be knocked over and broken. Also have ready a very small lamp.

Lead the group into the darkness and close the door. When they are quiet, give the following instructions. "We are going to play *Help Me*. You are to walk around. When you touch someone, take their hand and ask, 'Help me?' If they answer with the same question, drop hands and go on to another person. One person in the group has been secretly told to be the helper. If you grab his or her hand and ask 'Help me?' he or she will lean close and whisper, 'I will.' You then become a part of the helper. You continue holding hands with them. If someone bumps into you and asks, 'Help me?' you then lean close and whisper, 'I will.'" This continues until the whole group has joined hands. If the game goes quickly, it can be repeated.

Understanding I | *Everyone has a weakness or struggle.*

A Deeper Discovery of One's Weakness

(Estimated time: 20 minutes)

Once the group has finished playing, *Help Me*, turn on the small light. Have the young people remove their blindfolds. If possible, have everyone lie down on the floor. If there is not enough room, have the group sit and get as comfortable as they can. Once they are settled, explain that everyone is going to take a fantasy trip as a way of looking at some of their weaknesses.

1. Begin by having the youth close their eyes and keep them closed. Invite everyone to relax and to take seven or eight deep breaths. The calmer and gentler tone of voice used for the instructions, the better.

2. Ask the youth to concentrate on their bodies and try to locate any place that feels tense. Encourage them to relax this part of their body by imagining the tension running from this place through their arms and legs out the tips of their fingers and toes.

3. Once people are relaxed, lead them through the following fantasy. Go slowly through the instructions and let their imaginations do the work. Begin the fantasy by saying, "We are going to take a trip. Imagine you are out walking in the woods. Think about where you are . . . about the time of day . . . about the weather . . . about what the woods look like. Up ahead in your pathway you see a cave. It looks scary but exciting. You decide to go in. Try to picture what the cave looks like. Is it cold and wet? There is a pathway in the cave you can barely see. It leads deeper inside and into the darkness. You continue along the path. Far off in the darkness you can see a box. You know that the box has something to do with you. In fact, inside of it is something connected with a struggle you've been having lately. You come to the box. You open it. What do you see? It may be a picture of someone, a letter with a message for you, or an object. What is the object? What does the message say? Try to picture what is in the box. You look at it. It may be scary, but somehow seeing it makes it not so bad. You can put whatever it is back in the box, or you can take it with you if you like, but now it's time to leave the cave. You make your way out of the cave. Now you are back in the woods . . . and walking home." Be sure to go very slowly through the description of the fantasy and take some time.

4. Tell the group to take several deep breaths, and when they are ready, to sit up, and open their eyes.

God's Word on Weakness
(Estimated time: 20 minutes)

After the fantasy, have people find a partner. You will be asking the pairs to share themselves in more than a surface manner. It is best to let them choose friends or people with whom they are comfortable. Have the partners sit knee to knee. Distribute pencils and paper to each person.

Let someone in the group read 2 Corinthians 12:7–8.

Next, ask the youth to share with each other a struggle or weakness that they are facing now, like the Apostle Paul. It may be the one seen in the fantasy but not necessarily. On a piece of paper have each person answer the following questions about their weakness and discuss them with their partner:

Who is involved in the struggle or weakness?

What is it?

Where does it happen?

When does it happen?

Why does it happen (if applicable)?

When the conversation is complete, partners link arms or hold hands and move from the darkness into the light by going back into their regular meeting area. Make certain people bring the page that tells about their weaknesses.

Understanding II | *God's grace is sufficient.*

Support in Dark Times

(Estimated time: 15 minutes)

After the participants arrive, talk for a moment about how we sometimes have strength to do things that we cannot do by ourselves with the support of others. Demonstrate this by having the pairs sit back to back and lock elbows. Then ask them to try to stand up while keeping their elbows locked, without touching their hands or knees to the floor. This can be done as each partner pushes against the other. It is also fun to try this with four people, then eight, then the whole group. Next read 2 Corinthians 12:9.

Give people two 3" × 5" cards. Explain to them that on one "postcard" they are to write a message to their partner about the weakness or struggle that the partner has shared. On the other postcard they are to write an imaginary message from God to their partner about the struggle. Once these have been completed, partners share them with each other.

Understanding III | *Struggles give growth.*

Growth in Struggle

(Estimated time: 10 minutes)

Begin by sharing this with the young people: "Often when we are faced with a struggle, you and I ask the wrong question. We ask, 'God, why are you doing this?' Perhaps a better question would be, 'God, how are you going to use this?' Use the back of the page on which you described your weakness to answer the question, 'God, how are you going to use this weakness?' five times."

THE GIVING BOOK

The pairs are to discuss their answers. In addition, you might ask the group to list the strengths found in their weakness or struggle, if they have any.

The Light of the World
(Estimated time: 15 minutes)

For the closing worship, move the group to the sanctuary and seat them around the communion table or altar in a circle. The sanctuary should be brightly lit. Candles are a good addition.

Have the group sing the song, "Amazing Grace." Encourage the young people to place their sheets in a pile on the table or altar as they sing the song. Next have someone read 2 Corinthians 12:7–9. Pause, and then add verse: 10.

Use the following litany:

> We are neither good nor bad, we are both.
> And because God loves us, let us love ourselves.
> We are neither strong nor weak, we are both,
> And because God supports us, let us support each other.
> We are neither guilty nor innocent, we are both,
> And because God forgives us, let us forgive ourselves.
> We are neither perfect nor imperfect, we are both,
> And because God cares for us, let us care for each other.
> We are neither pure nor impure, we are both,
> And because God accepts us, let us accept ourselves.

Close with a group hug.

22

The Gift of Strength to Face Stress

A SENIOR HIGH ACTIVITY
FOR FINDING STRENGTH
TO FACE STRESS

Materials Needed

Items for team games (hard-boiled eggs, spoons, etc.)

Typing paper

Pencil for each person

Color-coded labels or red, green, and yellow markers

Index cards (five for each participant)

Bibles

Copies of statements for "Lilies of the Field"

Flower for each person

We are anxious, stress-filled people in need of God's peace. Whether pale and illusive or dark and foreboding, the shadows of worry are strangers to none. We often think of stress as an adult malady, but nothing could be further from the truth. It affects us all. Young people worry about acceptance, appearance, disagreement with parents, deadlines for school, work, and other issues. When left unchecked, stress is debilitating as well as essentially irreligious in character. What is our response to this needless and useless endeavor? How can Christians appropriately cope with stress?

Some people plant a border of marigolds around their tomato gardens to keep out the bugs. Amazingly it works. Something about the flowers prevents pests from destroying the fruit of the soil. We need marigolds to keep back the destructive influences of stress and anxiety waiting to invade the heart. A good devotion time or a phone call from a far-away friend can preserve one's sanity. A moment of silence, the sharing of a concern, and speaking the truth in love are all marigolds of different hues.

Jesus tells us not to worry about earthly things because God will provide for us (Matt. 6:25). We are no less than the lilies of the field or the birds of the air whom God clothes in splendor and feeds in abundance. We are reminded again and again of God's sustaining grace. This chapter shows the way we gain and lose sight of God's providence. Perhaps it will help you find creative avenues for coping with anxiety. The seeds of new habits, like marigolds, require nurture and work after planting to come to life. But if you are diligent, the efforts will be worth it. For it is not a garden we bring into being but a kingdom.

Games of Stress—More or Less

(Estimated time: 20 minutes)

Begin the activity by playing several different games. Pick games which offer a wide variety of stress levels. Have a relay such as the egg-in-the-spoon race. Divide the group into two teams. Give each team two spoons and an unshelled, boiled egg. Each team member carries the egg in the spoon past a certain point and returns. The egg is then passed into the spoon held by the person next in line. This person then goes past the point and returns. At no time can the egg be touched by anything but a spoon, and if the egg falls from the spoon, the group is automatically disqualified. The team that has all its members carry the egg past the point and back first wins. Musical chairs would be an appropriate alternate.

Next have the two groups make human pyramids. Encourage them to come up with as many creative kinds of pyramids as possible. For a third game, play hug tag. People are safe from whoever is "it" only while they hug someone else. After finishing, ask the groups if any of the games caused them to feel stressful. See if they have any ideas why or why not a game causes stress. One or two people in the group may ordinarily not participate in games when given the choice. If this is the case, ask them to share why they chose not to play. Explain that stress is the focus of the afternoon's activity.

Understanding I | *Life has many stressful situations.*

Stressful Situations

(Estimated time: 15 minutes)

You will need ten sheets of paper, each with a number from one through ten on it. Tape the numbers on a wall from smallest to largest, making a continuum from one to ten. Use the following list of situations. Have group members stand along the continuum to reflect the stress they would feel in the given situation. One would represent no stress and ten would be a highly stressful situation.

STRESS SITUATIONS

1. Talking in front of a group
2. Attending the first day of classes in a new school
3. Being at the free-throw line at a basketball game
4. Studying for a test
5. Applying for a job
6. Talking to one's family
7. Asking or waiting to be asked for a date
8. Going out with friends
9. Being alone
10. Being with people
11. Being called on in class

Understanding II | *We respond to stress in different ways with different levels of appropriateness.*

Traffic Light Discoveries

(Estimated time: 15 minutes)

Have red, green, and yellow markers, typing paper, and a pencil for each participant. In place of the markers you may use red, yellow, and green self-adhesive color-coded labels. Have people write down all the ways they deal with stress on the sheet of typing paper. Examples would include pouting, slamming doors, eating, crying, being alone.

Then ask individuals to color code their methods with the labels or markers when they have written as many as possible. Use green to indicate a healthy nurturing way of handling stress, yellow to indicate a method that is good with limitations (such as eating), and red as an unhealthy and nonnurturing way of handling stress. Count up the total of each color and talk about the

THE GIVING BOOK

results. Ask the young people, "What did you discover?" or, "What do you need to change?" or, "What methods would you keep?"

Responding to Stress
(Estimated time: 10 minutes)

Give each participant five index cards for this activity. Have them write a stressful situation on each card and then rank the cards from least to most stressful. Then encourage people to put down a normal response for each. Next, have them write as many new and creative responses to the stressful situations as possible. Talk about the results. See if any discoveries were made.

Understanding III	*Because God has provided for us, we are not to be anxious.*

"Lilies of the Field, Birds of the Air"
(Estimated time: 20 minutes)

Give people Bibles, pencils, and sheets of paper with these statements on it:
1. Right now the most stressful thing for me is . . .
2. I am like the lily or the bird because . . .
3. God cares for them by . . .
4. God cares for me by . . .

Tell the group to read Matthew 6:25–33 and meditate in silence for thirty minutes. Encourage individuals to go off by themselves for the quiet time. The important thing is to have the time of quiet, calm, and meditation. Also ask people to write a single sentence prayer during their meditations to be used in closing worship.

After the time is completed, gather the group and discuss the experience. See who found it restful and who found it stressful.

Worship
(Estimated time: 10 minutes)

Have a flower for each person. Gather the group in a circle. Offer the sentence prayers that have come from the quiet time. Go around the circle and face each person. Say to them, "Consider the lilies of the field. The Lord will bless you. The Lord will keep you. The Lord will give you peace." Then give each person a flower and a hug.

23

Christmas: Only the Beginning of God's Yes

A WORSHIP ACTIVITY
FOR CHRISTMAS

Materials Needed

A box of junk—wood scraps, twigs, straw, hammers, nails, etc.

Enough nails for each person

Red construction paper hearts, with yarn attached

Song books or sheets

Bread and wine (if communion is celebrated)

Christmas outshines the other holidays and holy days we celebrate. There are reasons for this, even beyond Christmas' obvious commercial appeal. Christmas has at its center an innocent Child. Adults project on the Child their gentle, sentimental, and self-conceived hopes. The Child lies helpless to respond. We imagine the Baby to be whatever we need, and no one is the wiser for it. Listen to the one-sided conversations that adults invent when talking to infants. We do this on a much grander scale with the Christ Child in the soft glimmer of millions of Christmas candles. Truly, as the carol says, the "hopes and fears of all the years are met in thee tonight."

Easter is another matter entirely. The center of focus is on a grown man who calls for life-shattering change instead of a baby who asks little. The response of Easter people is not as simple as Christmas people. What do we do when facing One who no longer sees us with the vision of innocence but from knowing eyes that see all and still choose to love, even unto death? For a faith that grows and offers nourishment, both views must be kept in tension. Those who celebrate God's coming to us in innocence are stretched. They are seen by the eyes of the Christ that look beneath every surface. Those who know too well the cries of anguish need to hear once more the music of the Babe's cry. God comes to us with outstretched hands, whether to instinctively clutch at a little finger, or to offer the weight of a cross. Our vision is far less myopic when to remember one, we remember both.

This Christmas celebration creatively combines the cradle and the cross. Through Scripture, insights, and activities, young people will see the timeless birth of Jesus in the context of all his life, while remembering their own past, present, and future.

Use this worship service as an evening's activity or, better still, in conjunction with a fellowship Christmas party. When you finish, exchange gifts, serve refreshments, or promote informal time to talk. For a change of pace and place, meet in someone's home. This service is best held around a fireplace.

Understandings	*We have fallen short of the glory of God.* *God forgives us and loves us still.* *Christmas calls us to remember all of Christ.* *Christ is alive among us.*

Getting Started

Gather in a circle for Christmas carols. Take time to sing the group's favorite songs for the season. If you are using a fireplace, form a semicircle around it. In the center of the group, place a pile of "junk." The junk should include wood scraps, twigs, cardboard, straw, anything flammable. This seemingly inappropriate Christmas centerpiece will supply the materials needed for the worship celebration. Let the curiosity mount. Listen for comments among the group about the junk.

Christmas: Only the Beginning of God's Yes

Everything's a Mess

(Estimated time: 15 minutes)

Begin with a prayer. Ask God's blessing on this Christmas celebration. Talk about reactions to the "junk." Ask participants to share their feelings or what they think the pile means.

Choose a leader and a reader for the next activity. A leader's part is written, but the leader should feel free to adapt it to whatever he or she would feel comfortable saying.

LEADER: The world's in a mess. Sometimes it seems like my family and most of my friends have problems. Sometimes I'm in a mess. This mess in the center of us symbolizes the mess that we sometimes make of our own lives. Life started going haywire, I expect, when sin entered the world.

READER: Genesis 3:14–19 [R.S.V.] is God's judgment after the fall:
"The LORD God said to the serpent.
'Because you have done this,
   cursed are you above all cattle,
   and above all wild animals;
upon your belly you shall go,
   and dust you shall eat
   all the days of your life.
I will put enmity between you and the woman,
   and between your seed and her seed;
he shall bruise your head,
   and you shall bruise his heel.'
To the woman he said,
'I will greatly multiply your pain in childbearing;
   in pain you shall bring forth children,
yet your desire shall be for your husband,
   and he shall rule over you.'
And to Adam he said,
'Because you have listened to the voice of your wife,
   and have eaten of the tree
of which I commanded you,
   'You shall not eat of it,'
cursed is the ground because of you;
   in toil you shall eat of it all the days of your life;
thorns and thistles it shall bring forth to you;
   and you shall eat the plants of the field.
In the sweat of your face
   you shall eat bread
till you return to the ground,
   for out of it you were taken;
you are dust,
   and to dust you shall return.'"

THE GIVING BOOK

LEADER: Yes, we are a mess. But God said "yes" to our mess. Even as early as in Genesis, and throughout the Old Testament, God promises to deliver us. Jesus is our deliverer. Jesus is God's "yes."

At this point, have the group sing a song. One good one would be "And God Said Yes" from the *Praise the Lord* songbook, published by Concordia Publishing House. Otherwise, use an appropriate Christmas carol like "Come, Thou Long Expected Jesus" or "Angels from the Realms of Glory."

READER: In 2 Corinthians 1:20–22 [RSV] we read: "For all the promises of God find their Yes in him. That is why we utter the Amen through him, to the glory of God. But it is God who establishes us with you in Christ, and has commissioned us; he has put his seal upon us and given us his spirit in our hearts as a guarantee."

LEADER: So to clean things up, God sent his son to make things right between God and us. Because of this, we are free to come before our Lord and confess our "mess."

Confess the Mess

(Estimated time: 15 minutes)

Have people take a wood scrap or twig from the pile of junk. Allow a moment for reflection. Ask participants to think of a one-word confession. It might be something they are struggling with, such as a misunderstanding, anger, impatience, someone they are unable to forgive. Go around the circle and as individuals say their word, have them toss the wood scrap into the fire. (If you do not have a fire, collect the scraps in a paper bag or box and remove them after everyone has finished.)

Celebrating the Joy of Forgiveness

(Estimated time: 15 minutes)

LEADER: Things did look dim, but now there's a glimmer of hope. And it's not just a glimmer—there's a bright and beautiful light!

READER: Isaiah 9:2–3 [RSV] tells us:
"The people who walked in darkness
   have seen a great light;
those who dwelt in a land of deep darkness,
   on them has light shined.
Thou has multiplied the nation,
   thou has increased its joy;
they rejoice before thee
   as with joy at the harvest,
   as men rejoice when they divide the spoil."

LEADER: In the light of God's forgiveness, we have peace. As a sign of our joy, let us share the peace of Christ with one another by giving hugs.

Sing "Hark, the Herald Angels Sing."

LEADER: The plan and picture are beginning to look clearer. God works in our lives in ways that are unpredictable. God continues to surprise us.

An Instrument of Salvation

(Estimated time: 15 minutes)

Take nails and give each person two to tap together as rhythm instruments. Sing "Listen to My Heart Song" in *Songs* by Johann Anderson. If this song is unfamiliar, use "Good Christian Men, Rejoice" or another appropriate Christmas carol, but be sure to choose one that has a fun beat. Sing and play "nail instruments."

LEADER: God's plan of salvation in life for us involved more than a birth. It includes a death—the death of Jesus. Look at the nails you hold. For Christ they became instruments, instruments of death. Jesus was nailed to the cross for us. He shared our struggles.

READER: Just as the prophet Isaiah said,
"Surely he has borne our griefs
    and carried our sorrows;
yet we esteemed him stricken,
    smitten by God, and afflicted.
But he was wounded for our transgressions,
    he was bruised for our iniquities;
upon him was the chastisement that made us whole,
    and with his stripes we are healed.
All we like sheep have gone astray;
    we have turned every one to his own way;
and the LORD has laid on him
the iniquity of us all.
He was oppressed, and he was afflicted,
    yet he opened not his mouth;
like a lamb that is led to the slaughter,
    and like a sheep that before its shearers is dumb,
    so he opened not his mouth.
By oppression and judgment he was taken away;
    and as for his generation, who considered
that he was cut off out of the land of the living,
    stricken for the transgression of my people?
And they made his grave with the wicked
    and with a rich man in his death,

> although he had done no violence,
> > and there was no deceit in his mouth"[Isa. 53:4–9, RSV].

LEADER: We can see beyond the pain because we know the victory Christ brings.

Building a Stable

(Estimated time: 15 minutes)

LEADER: As we celebrate Christmas, the whole life of Jesus is remembered. Jesus' story begins in a stable. Let's take the wood, a reminder of the cross; nails, a reminder of his suffering and death; the straw, a reminder of his humbleness and lowly beginnings; and the cardboard, a reminder of the ordinary, and build a manger scene."

With the "mess," construct a creative stable scene. Use hammers and nails to help. Leave the manger empty. Make sure the manger scene is movable. You may wish to display it somewhere at church during the Christmas season. While you are building, sing "Away in a Manger," and "Gentle Mary Laid Her Child" or other manger melodies. When the stable and scene are completed, the reader continues.

READER: The story of that first Christmas is found in Luke 2:1–20: "In those days a decree went out from Caesar Augustus that all the world should be enrolled. This was the first enrollment, when Quirinius was governor of Syria. And all went to be enrolled, each to his own city. And Joseph also went up from Galilee, from the city of Nazareth, to Judea, to the city of David, which is called Bethlehem, because he was of the house and lineage of David, to be enrolled with Mary, his betrothed, who was with child. And while they were there, the time came for her to be delivered. And she gave birth to her first-born son and wrapped him in swaddling cloths, and laid him in a manager, because there was no place for them in the inn.
And in that region there were shepherds out in the field, keeping watch over their flock by night. And an angel of the Lord appeared to them, and the glory of the Lord shone around them, and they were filled with fear. And the angel said to them, 'Be not afraid; for behold, I bring you good news of a great joy which will come to all the people; for to you is born this day in the city of David a Savior, who is Christ the Lord. And this will be a sign for you: you will find a babe wrapped in swaddling cloths and lying in a manager." And suddenly there was with the angel a multitude of the heavenly host praising God and saying,
'Glory to God in the highest,
and on earth peace among men with whom he is pleased!'

When the angels went away from them into heaven, the shepherds said to one another, 'Let us go over to Bethlehem and see this thing that has happened, which the Lord has made known to us.' And they went with haste, and found Mary and Joseph, and the babe lying in a manger. And when they saw it they made known the saying which had been told them concerning this child; and all who heard it wondered at what the shepherds told them. But Mary kept all these things, pondering them in her heart. And the shepherds returned, glorifying and praising God for all they had heard and seen, as it had been told them."

Jesus in Our Hearts

(Estimated time: 15 minutes)

LEADER: The manger is empty, for Jesus is not there. The joy is that beyond Jesus' birth, life, and death, he lives in us! Jesus is in our hearts.

At this point, celebrate holy communion if it is permissible in your tradition. Have each person share with the whole group by completing this sentence: "A joy I know because Christ is in me is. . . ."

Distribute red construction paper hearts with yarn attached so that they can be worn. As they are given, say _____(name)_____ "Christ is in your heart," Sing "Joy to the World" and emphasize the words, "Let every heart prepare him room."

Join hands and form a circle. Close with a prayer. With hands still joined, sing "Silent Night."

THE GIVING BOOK